The Art of Stepparenting

The Art of Stepparenting

How to Blend Families
Without
Tearing Them Apart

RICHARD R. RAMOS

Copyright © 2025 Richard Ramos

All rights reserved. The content contained within this book may not be reproduced, duplicated, or transmitted without direct written permission from the author or the publisher.

Published by The Ramos Group

ISBN (print): 978-0-9814714-3-3
ISBN (ebook): 978-0-9814714-4-0

Book design and production by www.AuthorSuccess.com

Praise for The Art of Stepparenting

With deep insight and empathy, Richard provides a roadmap for navigating the complexities of stepparenting. His guidance is not only practical but deeply transformational, empowering stepparents to lead with love, patience, and resilience. If you're blending a family, or come from one like I do, this book will be a trusted companion and guide.

–Richard Paul Morales, Executive Director of Latino Coalition for Community Leadership

I wish I had this book years ago! As a stepparent, I know the challenges all too well. Richard's insights have been invaluable in helping me understand the challenges we go through while providing real, practical solutions that work. Since reading this book, my stepson and I have been working through it together, and it's been a game-changer. This book does more than help blended families survive—it shows us how to truly connect and thrive. Richard's wisdom is a gift to anyone navigating the delicate dynamics of stepfamily life.

–Mercedies Escalante, Stepparent, Advocate for Blended Families, and Peacekeeper/Case Manager, Garden Pathways, Delano, CA

Stepparenting is one of the most challenging—and rewarding—roles a person can take on. Richard's book offers an invaluable resource filled with actionable insights and heartfelt encouragement. His expertise in family dynamics and youth development makes this a must-read for anyone seeking to build a harmonious blended home.

–Cheryl Polan, Founder & Executive Director, The Rock Found, Greely, CO

"In 2010, my wife Nikki and I opened our hearts and home to four foster children. Today, we have legal guardianship of three of them. Walking the path of fatherhood in a blended and complex family dynamic has been one of the most challenging—and rewarding—experiences of my life. Richard Ramos gets it. In this book, he shares

not just wisdom, but hard-earned, practical tools for building real connection, trust, and love as a foster parent and guardian. It's a guide that honors both the struggle and the beauty of forming a blended family. If you're stepping into this role, you don't have to do it alone—this book is a powerful companion."

–Juan Avila, Chief Operations Officer,
Garden Pathways, Bakersfield, CA

Hello, my name is Alan. I would like to share my testimony about how Richard's book, The Art of Stepparenting, and his Parents on a Mission program, has helped me become a better stepfather.

As a child, I suffered a lot of physical, verbal and mental abuse at the hands of my parents. Insults and beatings were a normal part of how I was raised. As a result of this, my mindset on how children are supposed to be raised was very damaged. This affected me very much when I married my wife who already had three children.

Richard has taught me how to break free from the damaged way that I believed children should be raised. Parents on a Mission (POM) has taught me how to be patient and calm with my stepchildren. I am now more kind and understanding of their needs.

I will always be grateful for POM and how it has helped me become a better stepfather and man. I recommend POM to any stepparent who desires a positive change.

Respectfully, Alan Alarcon

For

Armando Gonzalez, Anthony Ramos, Gina Ramos, Natalie Ramos, Sophia Ramos, Paul Ramirez Jr., Vincent Ramirez, and Jordan Ramirez

Thank you all for enduring us.

Free Offer

Watch our free mini-lesson: "Winning Their Hearts: How to Build Lasting Connection With Your Stepchild"

- A **one-part video masterclass** where I share how to cultivate trust, emotional safety, and authentic connection over time—not just survive under the same roof.
- Includes actionable strategies for fostering bonding moments, respecting emotional boundaries, and creating a sense of belonging.
- Perfect for stepparents feeling stuck, distant, or disconnected despite time together.

To access the free introductory gift video for all my readers. Visit: www.richardrramos.com

Contents

Introduction   1

Part One: Before the Blend—Understanding the Emotional Realities of Stepparenting   11

Chapter One: Unmatched and Unattached   13
Chapter Two: No Voice–No Choice   24
Chapter Three: Domestic Silence—Domestic Violence   35
Chapter Four: Mama Trauma   46
Chapter Five: Death. Divorce. Hope.   56
Chapter Six: The Stepdad Gap   65
Chapter Seven: The Blended Family Triangle   73

Part Two: POM Principles and The Stepparent's Role as a Transformational Leader   81

Chapter Eight: The POM Medal of Honor—Recognizing Your Worth as a Stepparent   83
Chapter Nine: Personal Growth for Stepparents—Managing Emotions and Expectations   87
Chapter Ten: Earning Respect as a Stepparent—Balancing Authority and Influence   111
Chapter Eleven: The Home Field Advantage—Building Strong Attachments That Counter External Influences   128
Chapter Twelve: Discipline with Love and Fairness—Avoiding the Authoritarian Style of Parenting   140
Chapter Thirteen: Community Building—How to Raise Productive Citizens   164

Chapter Fourteen: Reconciliation in Blended Families— 175
The Power of Forgiveness and Unconditional Love
Chapter Fifteen: How Stepparents Win Loyalty- 184
Leading Your Blended Family to Success
Conclusion: The POM Stepparent Mindset 207

Notes 210
Acknowledgments 214

Foreword

It's an honor to write this foreword for a book that speaks so deeply to the heart of what it means to build and nurture a blended family. Creating a blended family isn't easy—it takes courage, patience, and a whole lot of heart. But as this book beautifully shows, the rewards are incredible.

Stepparenting is a calling that demands both strength and tenderness. It's about building bridges where there once were gaps, forging new connections, and creating a sense of belonging that isn't defined by biology but by love, trust, and understanding.

The journey of blending a family is like tending a delicate garden. It takes time, faith, and a belief that even the toughest seasons will give way to growth. Every chapter in this book is a seed planted with care, offering guidance, hope, and the reassurance that you're not alone. The author masterfully blends practical advice with emotional depth, showing us that vulnerability and strength are not opposites; they are partners in creating deep, meaningful relationships.

What stands out most is the raw honesty with which the author addresses the ups and downs of this journey. There are moments of uncertainty, conflict, and doubt—but also small victories, unexpected joy, and quiet moments of connection that make every struggle worthwhile. The compassion woven through these pages is a powerful reminder that even when things feel hard, you're never alone.

I've witnessed firsthand how blending families can lead to remarkable transformations. Whether you're a stepparent seeking guidance, a biological parent working to foster harmony, or simply someone who finds inspiration in resilience, this book will resonate with you. It doesn't just celebrate the wins; it acknowledges the hard parts too, making it real, relatable, and deeply human.

One of the greatest gifts this book offers is the reminder that a blended family is not about perfection, it's about love, commitment, and the willingness to keep showing up. It's a masterpiece in progress—a work of art created through shared effort and heart.

The wisdom shared in these chapters isn't theoretical—it's lived experience. The practical advice, thoughtful insights, and heartfelt stories come together to form a powerful guide for anyone walking this path. This book will leave you feeling hopeful, grounded, and ready to embrace the complexity of your relationships with courage and grace. And it's not just for blended families, but for anyone looking to create deeper, more authentic relationships. I hope you find not only the wisdom you seek here, but also the courage to write your own story of resilience, connection, and love.

–Patty Aubery
Number one *New York Times* best-selling author, *Chicken Soup for the Working Woman's Soul* and past president of Chicken Soup for the Soul Enterprises, Inc.

Introduction

The family structure experience and how it can affect children towards delinquent behavior has been studied for well over one hundred years. In study after study on why children become delinquent, anti-social, and violent, social scientists have clearly concluded that the role of the family is at the root of the problem. These studies also show that children brought up in single-parent homes and stepfamilies are more prone to delinquent behavior than children raised by their biological parents[1], a fact that I believe is overlooked and deserves more attention to reverse this trend that contributes to unsafe communities.

Normally, the focus is simply on *parenting* or *the family* in general, but these studies confirm that in America today, single parenting, parents of divorce, second and third marriages, stepparenting, and blended family realities are the real, more pressing issues and challenges for families in need of support.

In her book, *The Good Divorce*, author Dr. C. Ahrons says that today's society is predominately made up of stepfamilies and recognizes there is a real need for specific training in the particular dynamics of stepfamilies and how they differ from the nuclear family experience. She also suggests that coaching stepfamilies using nuclear family comparisons can potentially be harmful for stepparents working through blended family dynamics.[2] Furthermore, according to the Pew Research Center 2023 study on The Modern American Family, the predominant American family form has undergone significant change, and Americans are experiencing a very different and diverse family life.[3]

The Hard Facts

The US Census Bureau report of "America's Families and Living Arrangements" estimates there were 10.9 million one-parent family groups with a child under the age of eighteen in 2022.[4] The study also showed that:

- It is predicted that 50 percent of children in the US will go through a divorce before they are eighteen.
- Sixty percent of all remarriages eventually end in divorce.
- One of three Americans is now a stepparent, a stepchild, a stepsibling, or some other member of a stepfamily.

These statistics have shown how these family realities contribute to a high rate of juvenile delinquency in one form or another, further emphasizing the need for a more intentional focus on single parents, blended families, and stepparenting for the sake of building safe communities in the twenty-first century and beyond.

In this book, I intend to share what I have learned from the literature on these family issues, my observations from the numerous high-risk single parents and stepparents I have worked with over the last twenty-five years providing counseling and parenting classes, as well as my personal experience of being a stepparent and blended family member for most of my adult married life.

Parents on a Mission

Parents on a Mission (POM) is a parent leadership curriculum I created to help the students who were on my caseload when I worked as the at-risk counselor for two years at a junior high school and two years at a high school from 1990 to 1994. My daily focus was listening to, encouraging, and mentoring the fifty students on my caseload. I continued in this way for my first year. It was rewarding to see that over time, I was winning my students' confidence and trust and seeing some results of troubled and unmotivated students begin to try and make positive changes in their lives. I created a club for Latino students and organized school dances and other after-school activities and field trips. We were making progress . . . but then I began to notice a trend. Many of my students began to go back to their old ways, ditching classes, not coming to school, failing to do homework, not passing their classes, and getting in trouble outside of school in the neighborhood. This became a frustrating roller coaster ride of ups and downs with individual students.

I wondered why my students, who seemed to be on the right track, were slowly beginning to go backwards. It was like watching a healthy flower begin to dry out, wilt, and die. At this point, I decided to see what was going on at home. I felt I needed to conduct home visits and listen to the parents of my students and get their side of things. That's when everything changed for me.

I decided that after my day at school, I would show up at their home (unannounced), introduce myself, and ask if I could have a few minutes to let the parents know who I was and what my role at the school was. My initial intention was simply to develop a relationship and build trust by having light, general conversations about their family, the school, my own family, and whatever other topics came up during our conversations. However, these home visits became an unexpected and eye-opening experience that changed my paradigm of how to help troubled youth.

The conventional method of dealing with problem youth is to focus our attention on the problems that the troubled and rebellious youth cause and counsel them by asking them why they are doing what they are doing; to listen and reason with them on why their choices of behavior are wrong, destructive, unacceptable, and, in the long-run, hurtful to their potential future. But after making enough home visits, I saw a different picture. I had one of those *aha* moments where a different light goes on and you see things more clearly. I then realized that I needed to change my focus from the problems troubled youth create to the problems that create troubled and rebellious youth.

During my home visits, I witnessed a lot of family dysfunction: lack of communication, lack of respect for parents, lack of control of their kids' whereabouts, lack of respect for authority, and other things that did not contribute to a healthy home environment. This is not to say each home was the same, but there were one or more factors that I could see were contributing to the anger, resentment, and sadness I was hearing from my students in my school office that was having a direct effect on their attitude and lack of performance in school.

I witnessed that when young people have experienced emotional trauma or have sad and angry hearts, there is no room for motivation to sit in a class, listen, learn, read, and study. I clearly understood that my focus had been placed on the wrong thing. It was like a young person who comes to you who is both starving and suffocating at the same time and force-feeding him to eat without first relieving their suffocation so they can breathe and then eat. It's not that they are rejecting the food they need, but rather they are unable to receive it because they can't breathe. If you've ever been out of breath from running or working out, you know what I mean. You can't drink the water you need until you catch your breath. I call this the *inside-out* approach versus the conventional outside-in approach to counseling. In this case, the inside-out approach needed to start inside the home with parents. As I have often said in teaching Parents on a Mission, we are losing more kids to suffocation than to starvation (metaphorically speaking).

This paradigm shift helped me realize that I was fighting a losing battle because no matter how much encouragement and counsel I was giving at school, these students were going home to an environment that was defeating and tearing down everything I was trying to accomplish. The more I thought about what I observed in their home life, the more I concluded that if I really wanted to help my students, the best thing I could do was to try to help their parents create a better home environment. Consequently, I started teaching the POM parenting classes.

Today, POM is being taught throughout the United States in several states and numerous cities, where I have trained more than 2,000 of what I call "POM Mentors" who teach the POM leadership curriculum I developed. Once these community leaders are certified as POM Mentors, they recruit parents in their respective communities through schools, churches, and nonprofits. POM is also being taught as a family reunification program throughout the Colorado Department of Corrections, Pennsylvania Department of Corrections, and has been the number one requested parent and family reunification program of the Kern County Sheriff Department in the county jail in Bakersfield, California, since 2015. Additionally, in 2022, the City of Guatemala adopted POM as part of their violence prevention strategy, as well as the city of San Salvador, El Salvador in 2024.

Through my POM program I have witnessed the reconciliation of parent-child relationships and positive family transformation of hundreds of families from all different ethnicities, cultures, and religious backgrounds in nuclear, single-parent, and blended families.

The Mexican Brady Bunch

My first parent experience began as a stepparent in 1978. My wife at that time had a two-year-old child, my stepson, who, as of this writing, is now forty-nine years old. I don't like to refer to him (or my other stepsons) as a *stepchild*, because somehow that term implies something missing and negative in the relationship. But I guess that's the thing about step/blended families—it's complicated. And since that is the subject that I will be addressing here, I will be using those terms interchangeably throughout the book.

I married my current wife, Christina, in 2002, and together we formed a blended family of eight children—my five (two sons and three daughters) and her three sons. At the time, four of them were still teenagers, and the youngest was just five years old. Needless to say, blending our families came with its fair share of challenges. As stepparents, we've navigated difficult moments, learning and growing through the process. Yet, despite the struggles, we deeply cherish the relationships we've worked so hard to build with each of our children.

When I use words like "challenges," "difficult moments," and "struggles," I'm referring to us—the parents—not our children. These difficulties stem from the immature (and selfish) decision we made to get married and blend our families, forcing our kids to accept and adapt to a situation they neither asked for nor wanted. Their rebellion, defiance, and resistance were not only expected but justified. However, knowing it was inevitable didn't make it any easier. And notice I said "doesn't"—because even after all these years, we are still working through some of the lingering emotional effects that naturally come with blending families.

If you were to meet the Ramos/Gonzalez/Ramirez family today, you would probably be encouraged, and maybe even impressed, by the way in which we get along, enjoy each other's company, and express our love for one another. However, that's looking from the outside in.

From the inside out, everything I shared above is real and true—but it has come at a price. Through the hardships and lessons I've faced as a widowed parent, divorced parent, single parent, and stepparent, I hope to offer encouragement. My journey is proof that, despite the challenges, you too can experience the richness of stepparenting and create a healthy, happy blended family life.

To that end, I have structured this book into two parts. Part One explores some common challenges faced by single parents, stepparents, and blended families, particularly in relation to the potential risks of delinquency and violence among youth. In Part Two, I introduce the *Parents on a Mission* (POM) principles—guiding values that I advocate for all caregivers, including biological parents, stepparents, single parents, grandparents, foster parents, and any other parenting of children. These principles have been instrumental in fostering reconciliation, restoration, and transformation within families of all types. My goal is to extend the *POM experience* to you, offering insights that can help strengthen and heal your own family as you engage with this book.

After reading this book, you will:

- Learn why your family of origin history may hinder your capacity to connect with your stepchildren and how to overcome it.
- Understand how to reconcile strained and/or broken stepparent-child relationships back to the harmony of happiness.
- Learn how to win loyalty and earn respect for your authority as a single parent and stepparent.
- Recognize *stepfamily relational triangles* and how to avoid them.
- Be aware of what I call the "stepdad gap" and how to close it through growth in parental emotional maturity.

Although challenging, the single-parent, stepparent, foster-parent, and blended family experience can be done in a way that provides you with the richness of restoration, reconciliation, and harmony that all families deserve to enjoy.

Richard R. Ramos
Santa Barbara, CA

PART ONE

BEFORE THE BLEND

Understanding the Emotional Realities of Stepparenting

CHAPTER ONE
Unmatched and Unattached

Carl Panzram, a man most people have never heard of, tells his compelling story as one of many examples we gain insight from of how a child from a broken home became a man with a history of the most hardened, cruel, vile, grotesque, and sadistic life as recorded in his autobiography.[1] While awaiting his execution in a death row isolation cell in Washington D.C. in 1928, he asked for a pencil and lined paper to write out his own version of his life. Those who came across his path knew *what* he did, but he wanted it to be clear *why* he did what he did from his perspective.

Every night, he would push out the individual sheets of paper through the bars of his cell to the prison guard. On page after page, he freely and proudly admitted and detailed a career of murdering twenty-one people, committing thousands of burglaries, robberies, burning down churches, larcenies, and sexually abusing over a thousand men. All to which he offered no apology and stated he was not *the least* bit sorry for any of it. This was a man obsessed with a hunger to destroy and kill. For example, as he was impatiently waiting on his day of execution, he snarled and yelled at his executioner that in the time it was taking to put him to death, he could have murdered twelve men already and told the guard to *quit fooling around* and hurry it up.

Panzram, as he was referred to by those who knew him, writes about why he vowed from an early age to commit a litany of viciousness towards others. He never cared about reforming himself but was only obsessed with the thought of reforming those who would try to reform him by killing them. At the end of his autobiography he offered that if anyone would care to study his life of crime, they would find one consistent theme and motive for all the destruction of lives he gladly committed: He only did what he was taught to do by what others did to him, which was to prey on the weak, the meek, and unsuspecting because of the life lesson he learned that *might was right*.

This begs the question: How does a person become like this? How can one human being be so cruel, grotesque, and depraved of conscience to commit such evil acts of violent crime to other human beings? What happens to the innocent child at birth that causes, or produces, a Carl Panzram? Yet, sadly, Carl Panzram is only one of many serial killers and violent criminals who have preyed upon the weak, innocent, and unsuspecting in our society.

In her book, *How Children Become Violent: Keeping Your Kids Out of Gangs, Terrorist Organizations, and Cults*,[2] Dr. Katherine Siefert writes how she devoted thousands of hours in interviews of the most violent criminals. Some of those most infamous, familiar names in American lore: Ted Kaczynski, AKA, *The Unabomber*, Charles Manson, David Berkowitz, AKA, *Son of Sam*, and Ted Bundy, and a host of others. Of the many case studies conducted by Dr. Seifert, one common thread she found as a predictor of children who grow up to become violent criminals is the failure, at the infant to the two-year-old stage of life, to form an emotional attachment with their mothers, fathers, and or caregivers. When children are unattached, she says, to their parents and remain unmatched with another sufficient substitute caregiver, this *unattached and unmatched* condition is the link that often leads to individuals with no empathy for others or the ability to lead a normal and productive life in society. Of those children who are unattached and unmatched to parents, she found the common elements of serious childhood trauma, including neglect, emotional, verbal, and sexual abuse, and the experience of domestic violent upbringings. Dr. Seifert names this condition as "Disruptive Attachment" and describes it as one of the leading causes of children who become violent.

This condition of Disruptive Attachment, in my view, speaks to either a lack of understanding, or a lack of ability, of the parents. As important as this emotional attachment is, we certainly cannot expect an infant to be responsible for making, or not making, it happen. The infant is the needy, the dependent, the innocent party that must rely on the adult parent to make this connection as a continuation of life after the womb. While in the womb of a mother, the umbilical cord serves as a physical attachment of nourishment.

However, once this attachment is severed, it typically marks the beginning of the need for nourishment on an emotional level, which oftentimes is somehow disrupted and never made.

In her book, *The Drama of the Gifted Child*, author and psychologist, Alice Miller, writes of the vital importance of a newborn infant not to immediately being separated from the mother as is common in our Western culture hospitals. Miller emphasizes the time of birth as a time when a mother's instinct for emotional attachment is flourishing and the opportunity for bonding between the mother and newborn stimulates a feeling of oneness that, if not captured at this initial mutual time of intimacy, may be missed and become a serious emotional obstacle *right from the start*.[3]

This understanding provides some insight into the life of a man like Carl Panzram. He was the youngest of six children. When he was born, his parents were living a life of economic hardship, raising their children during one of the worst depressions in the country on a small farm in 1892. After giving birth to Carl, his mother was in poor health and could not give her newborn the needed attention for emotional security and stability. While Carl craved the infant attention for attachment from others, there was no one able to give it to him.[4] His parents divorced when he was seven years old. His father, a violent-tempered man, disappeared from their life, leaving his mother and older brothers and sisters to work on their small farm. As a young boy, he was physically abused and beaten by his older brother and anyone else that felt he wasn't behaving correctly. He was constantly deceived and kicked around. At age eleven, he figured he had had enough and decided to leave home. But he was soon caught, taken home, and nearly beaten to death. It wasn't long before Carl was sent off to reform school where he experienced more beatings as a method for training him to be a good, moral, upright citizen. As a runaway teen, he describes two incidents where he was gang raped by older men, and as an adult he describes a life of more of the same: numerous violent crimes, beatings after being caught escaping from prison, and committing crimes in prison until he was finally sentenced with the death penalty.

To be fair, I am not suggesting that every child, or even most children, who experience trauma, neglect, abuse, and abandonment will end up a violent criminal like Panzram or the other serial killers I have mentioned. There are many examples of children who grew up in these unhealthy, abusive environments and have many mental health issues but do not become violent murderers. Many overcome their trauma and go on to lead productive lives. Nevertheless, the connection between broken homes and youth who commit violent crimes has been a subject of research for decades. Whole communities, particularly in low-income, urban areas, are affected by youth crime and, although the research to understand its root causes is inconsistent, there is agreement that the broken home is a definite major contributing factor.[5]

In their book, (originally published in 1912) *The Delinquent Child and the Home*, authors Sophonisba Preston Breckinridge and Edith Abbot, share their findings after a ten-year study of Chicago juvenile court records and interviews with youth residents of state training schools. They found that the majority of formally identified delinquent youth had lived with a single parent, a stepparent, or were orphaned. In addition, the families lived in poverty and crowded homes, and the parents often lacked education or were involved in criminal behavior. They also reported how often family friction occurred in single and stepparent families, thus linking family structure to parent-child relations and conflict.[6]

We tend to take for granted that parents of their biological children will naturally give their newborns the affection they need. However, in my own experience as a child, that was not the case, and in my experience of working with families over my career, I've discovered that providing affection and emotional attachment with children doesn't come as easy for some as it does for others, especially for those parents who experienced trauma as a child and have not been able, or willing, to seek the needed help in order to get on the road to inner healing and emotional stability. Admittedly, this is a difficult, lifelong process that many parents in need aren't willing to pursue. Sadly, this unwillingness to grow in emotional healing and maturity is a main cause of dysfunctional parenting that is passed on from generation to generation.

If the biological parents of children sometimes miss the mark of providing the affection and emotional attachment needed, as in the case of Panzram, how much more difficult for stepparents to provide this missing link should they marry into a family of small children who are missing this emotional attachment? Or vice-versa, in the case where a single parent brings into their home and life of their children an adult who has a hidden history of abuse either as a victim or perpetrator, as described in some fairy tales as the proverbial 'wicked stepmother.' This scenario applies to single parents, stepparents, foster parents, stepfamilies, and blended families. In my own experience, in terms of my inability to provide affection, this was one of the challenges I faced. As a young stepfather, I had no idea about any of what I've written above. My love and motivation to marry the mother of my stepson had nothing to do with him or his needs as a two-year-old child of divorce. This is not always a matter of being *wicked* or mean as a stepparent, but mostly a matter of emotional immaturity and ignorance and putting oneself in a position you are not ready for. Neither my wife, nor her son, was ready for it either. His needs were not a priority, and only an afterthought after we got married. Now, we find ourselves living under the same roof on a day-to-day basis. This was instant family. Instant parenting from a stepparent position of which I knew nothing. Obviously, I knew she had a two-year-old son, but the reality of a three-person relationship wasn't exactly what I had in mind. We overlooked all that. It was all about *us* and the rest would just fall into place naturally. Or so we thought. For example, her son was used to sleeping with his single mom every night. Why wouldn't he? He was only two years old and a child of divorce. But now this strange man is in the bed, let alone the house, and he's not having it, and neither am I. Now, mom is caught in the middle of an *emotional triangle* (something I will address more in a later chapter) trying to take care of her relationship with two males and at the same time expecting (hoping) the adult male will build a relationship with the child by showing understanding, compassion, and affection for her child's needs.

I was not raised by an affectionate mother. My mother was not raised by affectionate parents. Consequently, I was uncomfortable when it came to affection. Even after we had our own biological children, I was uncomfortable showing them affection. Luckily, for my children, their mother and grandparents (of Sicilian origin), smothered our children with an abundance of love and affection. When I first witnessed this, it made me feel awkward and uncomfortable. I didn't know how to act. I was not used to that kind of display of affection.

This emotional incompetence on my part was affecting our young family. I was aware of it but didn't know what to do about it. I was being too harsh with my stepson: impatient, intolerant, incompetent. When he would leave to spend time with his father, I was relieved, happier, and in a better mood. But when he returned home, I would have to revert to *being a stepdad*, and the cycle would start all over again. This is not to say we didn't have fun times, laughter, and a relationship. We did. But it would be hard dealing with the roller coaster of investing in our relationship, and then he would leave again to spend time with his father. When he came back, it took him days to talk, or even look at and acknowledge me, and thus to learn how to be affectionate in this situation was difficult to say the least. But, of course, that was looking at the situation from my perspective. It took time for me to consider his and adjust my behavior.

Perhaps you are reading this and experiencing this same type of struggle. Your stepchildren may even be older or younger than two years old. You may, or may not, be dealing with an ex-spouse. Or, like me, being affectionate is not something you are comfortable with, yet after reading this chapter, you now realize how important forming this emotional attachment is and feel a little discouraged. However, it's okay. That's normal and good that it bothers you because that means you are listening to your heart. You are in tune with your conscience and that is the beginning of growth and change.

Though it takes time and practice, the good news is you can learn to become affectionate as I did and remain so today as the affectionate father and stepfather my children need (I will have more to say on this process in later chapters). Thus, what I am emphasizing in this book is the need for stepparents, foster parents, and caregivers (in addition to biological parents) to be educated and provided with more resources as a means of preventing stepchildren from becoming unproductive citizens and/or perpetrators of crime. I believe these outcomes from these various family structures, other than the nuclear family, deserve more attention, which is my motivation for writing this book. As the research shows, the Disruptive Attachment is common amongst children raised by stepparents who later become delinquent youth and adult violent criminals.

As we consider solutions and answers to the questions of how kids become violent, why kids become juvenile delinquents, and how to deal with youth violence and create safe communities, this may seem too simplistic. But I argue that the incompetency of parents and stepparents at the very early stages of a child's life is overlooked as a root of the problem of why some children, especially those from broken homes, single parents, and stepfamilies, become delinquent, violent, commit crimes, and end up filling group homes, foster homes, jails, and prisons.

While social scientists continue to research and study these problems to provide information, resources, and training for the many caring mental health professionals and social service workers dealing with youth offenders caught up in the justice system, we must also include parents. Parents of all types discussed here are in the best position to have a great positive impact on the children under their care, and as the children under the care of single parents, stepparents, and foster parents continues to grow as a normal American family experience, the same resources for social service workers are vital for parents as well.

Key Takeaways for Chapter One

- Early emotional attachment plays a crucial role in child development and behavioral outcomes.
- Stepparents must focus on building trust through patience, consistency, and emotional availability.
- Understanding a child's background and experiences can help bridge the emotional gap.
- Parents should work together to create a unified and supportive home environment.

Action Plan for Chapter One

1. **Reflect on Emotional Attachments:** Identify ways to strengthen emotional bonds with your stepchildren.
2. **Practice Active Listening:** Set aside time to engage in meaningful conversations with stepchildren.
3. **Establish Predictability:** Create a stable and consistent household routine to foster security.
4. **Be Patient:** Recognize that building trust takes time and allow relationships to develop organically.
5. **Engage in Shared Activities:** Plan activities that encourage connection and create positive family experiences.

CHAPTER TWO
No Voice-No Choice

Earlier, I referred to my current blended family as the *Mexican Brady Bunch*, which (for those of you unfamiliar with this reference) was a 1970s hit TV sitcom program. However, our experience has been far different from the TV version of the *Brady Bunch* blended family.

I would never do anything to intentionally hurt my children, and I know my wife feels the same way. And yet, that's exactly what we did by the choice we made.

Looking back now at the timing of our marriage, it's interesting to think about how we make these decisions, especially when you *know better*. But somehow, you decide to do that thing that is not in line with your values. In our case, we knew it wasn't the best thing, or the best time for our kids, but we decided to marry anyway, which caused us a lot of remorseful feelings, not because we regretted getting married (we knew our deep feelings for each other were genuine). Still, our remorse and regret was because of the deep love we have for our children. Eventually, we began to experience how our choice gave them no voice, and forced them into a blended family situation causing them trauma, pain, and anger. How could we do this? How does this happen?

There are several factors that go into the process of decision-making. For example, this is a subject that marketers and advertising agencies pour millions of dollars into studying to understand how people make purchasing decisions. They want to discover what determines how choices are made in order to influence the buying habits of consumers. The details of all the psychology associated with influence and decision-making are beyond the scope of what I'm discussing here except to say that our emotions are at the core of our decision-making. And sometimes (or should I say most of the time) our emotional decisions lead to regret.

I read the story of a young woman reaching out for help on an internet forum for stepparents and blended families. She shares how she is full of regret, resentment, and anger with herself. She shares how she can't sleep due to her unhappiness with the circumstances she got herself into against her better judgment.

In her early twenties, she met a young man with whom she fell madly in love. However, there was one seemingly small issue. He had a two-year-old daughter. At first, they weren't living together and even though he made it clear to her that his daughter would always come first, she felt she understood and figured it would all work out.

Wanting to move forward in their relationship and eventually move in together, they worked hard to save money so they could buy a home. A few years later, they reached their goal and bought the home of her dreams, except for one thing. She didn't want his daughter to live with them. However, she never said it out loud. Knowing this, she moved forward anyway. As time went on, as one might expect, she resented her decision and grew in resentment towards the stepdaughter and her boyfriend to the point where she wrote that becoming a stepparent had ruined her life.[1]

It was sad to read her story. Here she was reaching out, seeking advice about what to do since she was now stuck with a mortgage she couldn't afford to pay by herself, but no longer wanted to be in the stepparent relationship. In hindsight, it's easy to ask the question: If you knew you didn't want to live with his daughter and were already feeling resentful towards her because of always having to take a back seat to her, why did you make this choice? Paraphrasing her words, *I was so in love with this guy that I was willing to try and be a family.*

Love is a very powerful emotion only superseded perhaps by the emotion of fear. When one falls under the strength of the emotion of love, one can decide things or do things that one might not normally do, things that are out of character, or even beyond what one thought one was capable of.

In her case, because of falling in love, her regret was about buying a home with someone who had a kid she didn't want. In our case, it was hurting our children who had no voice, and therefore no choice, in having to deal with their new blended family. Our choice, combined with their no voice, had bigger consequences than we realized. No doubt a mistake, and yet, in most cases, unavoidable when two adults with children fall in love. I suppose that's the selfishness of being in love. Even when you know better, you move forward in your relationship regardless.

The Timing of Choice

How your new relationship came into being determines how others usually will or will not accept it. If you are a widow or widower for a fair amount of time, most people will recognize that finding a new life partner, lover, or spouse is a good thing for you and acceptable to them. But that may not be true for your children or the children of the other party regardless of how long it's been since you became single again, which discourages you from wanting to hear their voice.

I have a friend who became a widower. After being single again for over a year, he decided to start dating. At this point in his life, he was living alone, and all his children were young adults. Some married with children. However, when he announced to them that he was going to start dating a woman, they would not accept it and, as far as I know, to this day they still don't accept it though their mother has been gone for many years.

In the case of divorce, the same issue of time between how long you've been divorced and when you start a new relationship will be acceptable with some but not for others. Again, what others will think or say might help or hurt you, but it usually will not deter you from moving forward in the new relationship. But what about the kids? Should we deny ourselves and/or sacrifice our relational needs for the sake of our kids? Some say "yes;" others will say "no." It will be different for every individual case, but like us, many won't and don't (although I'm sure there are parents who do) and thus will face the fallout of the children having no voice or choice.

Another very common scenario is the single mother who is no longer in a relationship with the boyfriend, who is the biological father of her child or children. (This could also be true for a single father.) Eventually, she meets someone, and the newly formed couple moves in with each other, forming a stepfamily situation whether the kids like it, want it, approve of it, or not. And, unfortunately, this can happen more than once, forcing the kids to adjust multiple times to a new stepfamily dynamic.

The other factor here is the age of your children when this new relationship takes place. In general, if the kids are very young like infants and toddlers, the transition could be a smooth one because they are not cognizant of what is happening. At that age, they have no stake in the game as long as Mamma is a stable figure in their young life and meets all their emotional needs for attachment.

Nevertheless, if the ex-spouse or biological father is in the picture, that can become problematic as the kids grow older. I'm not suggesting that the biological father shouldn't be in the picture because most of the time that is still a very important relationship for the kids to have, but (depending on the disposition of the father in this new situation) it can also have a negative effect on your relationship having to deal with the stress and inconvenient, awkward scenarios in a variety of situations like birthdays, holidays, school, and sports activities, not to mention in-laws still wanting to actively be involved in the life of your children (which is also a good thing in most cases).

Thus, there are a variety of ways a stepfamily can come to be, but the point I'm stressing here is the fact that, for the most part, our children are left out of the decision of blending families or inviting into their lives a stepparent, and that could happen more than once. It's a vulnerable time for them, and most likely they are not ready for it. In some cases where there may be domestic violence, children feel relief when their parents separate, but for the most part they are most likely hoping their parents will reconcile. So, the children are hurt, jealous, betrayed, resentful, sad, or even angry. Thus, it's understandable that when their parents start–or want to start–dating again, they reject it.

Let's break this down. First, if you were to give your children a voice in the matter, what is the appropriate age to discuss this adult issue with them? Second, does giving them a voice mean you will or will not move forward in your new relationship? Is it up to them? Third, what is the conversation you have with your older (young adolescent or older) children vs. their younger siblings? Or should it be the same conversation altogether?[2]

The research gives no definitive answers to these questions. Every family-including the many different child personalities and maturity levels-are different and therefore will react differently no matter what method, formula, or advice you follow. However, there is ample general guidance given from different studies regarding these issues[3] but, in my view, much of it simply comes down to common sense. But, as the old saying goes, *common sense is not always common practice*, and therefore it's wise for parents to heed the common principles suggested by a variety of sources that include:

- Timing of when to introduce your new partner to your children.
- Validating whatever feelings your children have about this new person.
- Setting boundaries and clear expectations about how much time your partner will spend with your children.
- Plan quality time with your children to assure them of their priority to you even if you are beginning a new relationship.
- Slow is better than quick change in this new relationship.
- Limit overnights, if at all, with your new partner.

The key ingredient to these types of crucial conversations is the emotional maturity level of the parents and understanding how important listening to the voice of their children is regardless of what their feelings might be. Because the truth is, we are not talking with them to make the choice for us. But we are talking with them to hear their voice and allow them to express whether they like, don't like, or even agree with the new relationship.

The purpose is not to try and convince them to accept the new relationship. Neither is it to simply inform them of what's going to happen. Rather, the purpose in sitting with them is to show them my love, empathy, and respect for their feelings (good or bad) as well as my feelings for a woman who is not their mother. The mistake parents make is to not understand that a child's vulnerable voice of dissent, when challenged, is not a voice heard, but a voice silenced. Most children can *gradually* accept that they had no choice in how they feel about someone who is not their biological parent. But what they are resentful of is their voice on the matter not being heard or understood.

All the studies I reviewed encouraged this type of open and honest communication with the children. But, again, that assumes the parent has the emotional capacity to correctly broach this sensitive subject in the ways suggested. That's why children are often given no voice. These suggested methods of speaking with children about the new partner require a family culture that may have never existed. This open communication is a foreign concept to many parents. That type of parent accountability is awkward, uncomfortable, inconvenient, and many parents don't possess the needed capacity, let alone the desire, and therefore don't discuss their new relationship with their children. Or, if they do, but don't approach it with a high degree of emotional maturity, the conversation can quickly escalate into a heated and ugly argument that will amount to three or more steps backward in building a stepparent-blended family relationship. Thus, to say the best practices or formula for blending families is complicated is probably an understatement.

All that said, let me end on a positive, encouraging note.

A positive exception to the expected outcome of difficulty is expressed in the following story of a young man who says, *I grew up in A Broken Home, But It Shaped Me and I'm Blessed For It.*[4]

This young man has an uncommon and insightful perspective on growing up in a broken family. He shares that his parents never got along. When friends asked if he wished his parents were still together, his answer was an easy *no*—based on his experience, he couldn't imagine how they had married in the first place.

For him, the hardest part wasn't that his parents were no longer together, but rather the realization that their focus was more on getting back at each other than on meeting his needs—things like his school schedule, lunch money, clean clothes, and extracurricular activities often took a backseat.

Despite these challenges, he considers himself fortunate to have experienced a *broken home*. While others pitied him because his father remarried twice after divorcing his mother, he saw it differently. To him, it meant he had gained five more adults to support him, including his mother's boyfriend, who had been a steady presence in his life since he was five years old. He also felt blessed because he was no longer an only child—divorce had given him six new siblings. What was once a battle over attending two family Christmases became a juggling act between four. Yet, instead of feeling torn, he felt loved and supported.

Growing up in a blended family taught him that all families have struggles, but those struggles can be overcome through forgiveness. He also learned that blood isn't always thicker than water—sometimes, the chosen family can be just as strong. He admitted he wasn't sure who he would have become if not for his broken home.

That said, his story is the exception rather than the rule for children of divorce and blended families. But even so, it offers hope.

Key Takeaways for Chapter Two

- Children in blended families often feel they have no voice in family decisions, leading to resentment and emotional withdrawal.
- Effective communication is essential for integrating stepparents into a child's life.
- Stepparents should acknowledge and validate the emotions of their stepchildren, even when faced with resistance.
- The timing of introducing a new partner into a child's life significantly impacts their acceptance and adjustment.
- Open, age-appropriate discussions about family changes help children feel heard and respected.

Action Plan for Chapter Two

1. **Encourage Open Dialogue:** Create safe spaces for children to express their thoughts and emotions about the new family structure.
2. **Validate Feelings:** Acknowledge children's concerns and fears, demonstrating empathy and understanding.
3. **Gradual Integration:** Take time to establish relationships with stepchildren before assuming a parental role.
4. **Set Clear Expectations:** Define family roles, rules, and boundaries collaboratively to foster a sense of security.
5. **Respect the Past:** Honor the child's relationship with their biological parent while building new family traditions.

CHAPTER THREE
Domestic Silence–Domestic Violence

It's still a vivid memory when I think about my dad and my sister.

I was a young boy of four or five years old. Although I can't remember all the details that led to it, I do remember the tiny one-bedroom home and standing at the door of the bedroom watching my dad, mom, and sister. At first, I couldn't make sense of what was happening. There was a lot of commotion, yelling, and screaming. But then it came into focus what was going on: my dad was sitting on top of my sister, beating her with his fists and the telephone receiver (the old rotary phones that had a handheld receiver used to hear and talk into), and my mom was yelling and screaming at my dad and trying to pull my him off of my sister, but to no avail. I don't remember how long it lasted, or how it all finally ended, except for a vague memory of police and police cars.

My father was a veteran of World War II. My mother always told us that my dad was a good man but had returned from the war as a *different man*. That was her explanation of how he became an alcoholic, which was attributed to the domestic violence we endured from time to time as children, even though he no longer lived with us. Although I know my mother did the best she could, only many years later, after I became a parent myself, could I begin to appreciate how this must have traumatized and deeply saddened my mother, having to raise five children under the threat of the unpredictability of an alcoholic husband that she still loved.

The incident I described above finally caused us to become a broken, single-parent family. Yet, that didn't stop other violent incidents from occurring because although my mom would not allow my dad to live with us, she still did allow him to visit. I'm sure she was either hoping he would change or just wanted him to still be involved in the lives of his five children. But that didn't work out so well either because it didn't stop more violent incidents from occurring.

I recall another incident around the same when my dad still lived with us. I was sitting on the floor playing with my toys. My back was against a door that had little square glass windows as the front design. At this point, I was intimidated and scared of my dad. So, when he was talking to me and trying to get my attention, I ignored him. I don't remember what he said or why he was trying to engage with me. Maybe he was scolding me. Maybe he was telling me to do something. Or maybe he was just trying to have a simple conversation with me. But I just kept ignoring him. The next thing I know, I feel his hand on my forehead, and then . . . .Bam! Crash! And the sound of shattered glass as he shoved my head through one of the glass windows. The only thing I remember after that was my dad and mom picking little pieces of glass out of my head and my mom crying.

A year or two ago, as part of a writing exercise, I was asked to describe one of the happiest moments of my childhood. That question really stumped me. I thought, *hum ... describe a happy day or one of the happiest memories I had with my family*; it saddened me. Not because I never had any good times. I did. But most of the good times were when I was outside of my immediate family, not with my dad, mom, brother, and sisters. It was playing sports at the park. It was spending time with my friends at the afterschool playground, having sleepovers at my friend's house (I never wanted to invite them to spend the night at my house and neither did my mom), and spending the weekends at my grandma and grandpa's house with my cousins. But to come up with *happy days* at home with my family, I really had to think about it. It wasn't like a rush of thoughts came to my mind. Again, not because I never had any happy days, but they are not foremost in my mind. There's so much I don't remember, except for some of the incidents like the ones described above.

Nevertheless, after my mom had made my dad leave our home, I do remember one day, sitting outside with my brother and my mom and asking her, "Mom, when is daddy going to come back home?"

She put her arms around both of us, like a mother hen sheltering her chicks beneath her wings, and sadly said, *I don't know* and held us as the three of us wept together.

I can't speak for my brother and sisters because, even to this day, we have never discussed these things amongst ourselves. (I still don't know what prompted my dad to beat up my sister.) But for me, these (and other) different bouts of violence filled my heart with anger and resentment towards my father. But here's the thing: we never talked about it. At least nothing was ever said to me. No explanation. No counseling. No apology. Zero. Nada. It just was. And that is the important point I'm emphasizing here. When abused children are left to themselves to process, suppress, hide, and or bury the trauma, as I was, that ultimately is a recipe for them, when they become parents, to become perpetrators of violence and repeat the abuse, trauma, and/or crime in their home.

Fortunately, not every child of domestic violence and abuse becomes a perpetrator of violent crime or an abusive parent or stepparent. I would venture to say that most abused children don't go that way. But that doesn't mean their traumatic victimhood goes away. It's just suppressed and eventually expressed in different ways. Although I thankfully did not become a hardened, violent criminal, I did have a lot of anger and resentment that caused a mean streak, temper, and penchant for getting in fist fights at different times, with different people, in different places. Most of that, of course, took place in my youth and younger adult days. But I never really thought about it or considered it a problem . . . until I became a stepparent, which, as I mentioned earlier, was my first parenting experience. That became a wakeup call that I didn't even realize I needed because I didn't know I was *asleep.*

Effects of Our Family of Origin

This is the point I am making: biological and stepparents alike who had the unfortunate experience of some type of abuse and/or witnessed domestic violence, and have never dealt with their childhood trauma, now have kids and/or stepkids in blended families, and that oftentimes becomes a potential repeat of child abuse and domestic violence.

In her book, *Breaking Down the Wall of Silence: The Liberating Experience of Facing Painful Truth*, world-renowned psychotherapist Alice Miller, asks the question: How can a woman be a mother to her children until she has mothered the neglected, abused, mistreated child she herself had been?[1]

This is one of the root causes of community crime and violence but overlooked and explained or excused away. This combination of abused children who become parents and stepparents and have not had the opportunity, or sought the opportunity, to heal themselves of their past unresolved wounds, creates the potential for an ongoing vicious generational cycle of victimizing children, some of whom become a menace to society[2]

In my book, *Parents on a Mission: How Parents Can Win the Heart, Mind, and Loyalty of Their Children*,[3] I challenge parents with the question: where do the citizens of the community come from? Citizens go to school. They don't come from school. Citizens go to church. They don't come from church. They go to work. They don't come from work. Thus, the question is, what kind of citizens are we sending into the schools, neighborhoods, and communities every day? And

I believe the same question applies here, as does the answer: where do the criminals of the community come from (and I count parents and stepparents that abuse their children amongst the worst kind of community criminals)? Ultimately, they come from the home.

My epiphany of my need for help with my resentment, temper, and anger came to me one day as a very young husband and stepfather. My wife and I were having one of our rare arguments. As we continued to yell and scream at each other, I could feel that violent streak I had welling up inside of me. If you've ever experienced this, it's that moment when you lose yourself in anger. You lose the ability of your mind to think first. You are now under the control of the raw, blind emotion of rage that strikes out verbally, and/or physically, not caring in that moment about the potential consequences. That's what happened to me. An emotional loss of control that was familiar to me, but this time it was with my wife, and then, whap!! I slapped my wife. And as quickly as I slapped her, I became ashamed and devastated, realizing what I had done.

Psychological theories abound as to how and why this type of human (inhuman?) behavior happens. My theory about acts of violence has always been that they are the result of an angry heart, and an angry heart is the result of unresolved injustices that usually take place in the home. I've never had my theory affirmed until I read books by Alice Miller (mentioned above), who suggests that parents and stepparents who abuse their children are acting out their revenge towards their abusive parents on their children. And this is because they were taught never to question their parents. To do so was tantamount to a sin, and therefore children were just to accept the abuse, neglect, and mistreatment. If they were to question anyone as to why they were being mistreated, they should blame themselves as deserving even though they could never understand the reason for it. Furthermore, she explains that some of history's most infamous and ruthless, totalitarian, fascist dictators like Hitler, Stalin, and Ceausecu, became the murderous monsters as a result of never dealing with their traumatic, abusive childhoods and thus taking out their revenge against their parents by slaughtering millions of innocent lives (quite a claim).[4]

I never hit my wife again, and I never physically abused my stepson. But as our family grew, I did have to come to grips with my anger, short temper, intolerance, impatience, and sometimes cruel ways of reacting to my stepson, and later, my own children's behavior. As I searched my heart, I finally began to discover that the root of my anger was a result of my own resentment and unresolved issues with my dad, who had already passed away several years earlier. But somehow, during this time of soul searching, I realized that a dead man was controlling my life. It was like a revelation by the grace of God, and in those moments, I knew that if I wanted to be free from the grip of a man in a grave, that I needed to forgive my father and let the past go. Thus, in that broken condition of tears, that is exactly what I did. And from that moment on, I could now become the husband and father that my family both needed and deserved. It didn't happen overnight, but it did happen, and continues to happen, as I continue to work on and grow myself in emotional maturity.

This is my hope for all stepparents reading my story and the other stories I share in this book. Together we can make a huge difference for the betterment of the stepparent, blended family experience. But the key is that we must start with ourselves and be willing to face some hard truths of our past about our own parents if we are to move forward and continue to break down the silence of domestic violence.

Child abuse is an ancient, worldwide crime that continues to this day. Domestic silence about domestic violence has been historically common, encouraged, and an accepted way of ignoring it, even amongst the *experts* of psychoanalysis, psychiatrists, psychotherapists, social workers, counselors, and teachers. Current reports indicate that only 1 percent of these crimes are reported annually, and that is a crime in itself. In addition, recent studies have shown that children living in single-parent households are more likely to experience, witness, or become victims of domestic violence than children living with their biological parents.[5]

As a case in point (as of this writing), the three-year-old daughter of a friend of one of my stepsons, was killed by the boyfriend of the mother. The boyfriend had apparently been physically abusing the child, yet no one said anything until it was too late. The autopsy report showed the child's death was caused by the trauma from a blow to her head.

These sad and sick tragedies happen far too often, and though it's hard to talk about, we need to talk more about it because, as in the case of this innocent three-year-old girl, she became the forgotten child and victim with no one to turn to for help. This type of abuse in single-parent homes then becomes another vicious cycle of hidden trauma. In addition to the single-parent household's potential for domestic violence, the same risk factors (if not more so) apply to the blended family household. Stepparents (not all of course) are notorious for abusing their stepchildren.[6] The increased risk of neglect, physical, and sexual abuse of children by their stepparents can be due to a number of factors. But the main factor seems to be a history of their own domestic violence as children, and the lack of the appropriate opportunity, and desire, to apply sensitive coping mechanisms to deal with their own pain.

Ending The Conspiracy of Silence

As mentioned earlier, Alice Miller speaks extensively to the fear and lack of courage adults who were victims of child abuse have to face the truth about their abusive parents. She claims that had this not been the case it could have saved so many children from abuse that contributes to their becoming threats to society. Her contention is that this has been an ongoing conspiracy of silence about abusive parents popularized by Sigmond Freud, who refused to acknowledge his own child abuse, and rather created his theory that the cause of neurotic children was a result of their own sexual inhibitions, which only served to place the focus, blame, and burden on the child for healing, and hide the fault of abusive biological and stepparents[7]

Given the fact that the single-parent and blended family household has become a normal American family structure, where much of the abuse of children is occurring and yet, as mentioned earlier, only 1 percent of the modern-day abuses of children are reported, this must change.

Therefore, my goal and hope here is to bring more attention and a more encouraging light to help stepparents find their way to the healing they need. Through Parents on a Mission (POM), I hope to enlighten a mindset of fear to one of safety, understanding, empathy, and compassion for what stepparents may have suffered as children that has never been addressed and resolved with peace. As I repeatedly say, POM is not about focusing on how we can fix our children and stepchildren. It's about how we parents/stepparents can fix ourselves. It's not about focusing on the problems rebellious stepchildren create, but rather, it's about focusing on the problems that create rebellious children and stepchildren. Furthermore, it's not about *blaming* stepparents, but rather about *naming* stepparents (in combination with biological parents) as the number one asset in the lives of their stepchildren, and therefore the most important people in the community since stepparents and blended families are no longer the exception but a very normal part of American society and therefore hold the future of our society in their hands.

Key Takeaways for Chapter Three:

- Domestic violence and childhood trauma have lasting effects on emotional well-being and future relationships.
- Stepparents may unknowingly carry unresolved emotional wounds into their new family dynamics.
- Recognizing and addressing past trauma is crucial for creating a healthy and supportive home environment.
- Open discussions about family history can help children and stepparents process their emotions constructively.
- Healing from past wounds requires intentional emotional growth and support from loved ones.

Action Plan for Chapter Three:

1. **Identify Emotional Triggers:** Reflect on past experiences that may influence parenting and stepparenting styles.
2. **Seek Healing:** Engage in therapy, support groups, or personal development resources to address past trauma.
3. **Create Safe Conversations:** Encourage open discussions with stepchildren about their emotions and past experiences.
4. **Foster Emotional Security:** Establish a home environment that prioritizes emotional safety and mutual respect.

CHAPTER FOUR
Mama Trauma

Is it possible for a mother not to love her newborn baby? To not feel emotionally connected to her innocent infant son or daughter? Apparently, the answer is yes, according to Peg Streep, Author of *Mean Mothers: Overcoming the Legacy of Hurt*[1]

As astonishing as it may seem, Streep says the expectation that all mothers automatically are emotionally connected, attached, and feel love for their child is a myth. It's a taboo subject that few mothers want to admit, let alone talk about. In Streep's case, she shares how she realized her own mother did not love her as early as the tender age of three or four. But this was not apparent to others because her mother was very good at hiding it when around her father, family, and others. But her mother's lack of love for her wasn't because her mother had no capacity to love. That became obvious later with the birth of her brother. She watched her mother give him all the love he needed. This increased her confusion, deepened the hurt, and increased the intensity of blaming herself, and repeating all the obvious questions she had already been asking (but had to keep to herself): *why not me? What's wrong with me? What did I do—or what am I doing—to not deserve my mother's love?*

These are just a few of the thoughts and emotions of children rejected and neglected by their mothers. But how else can a child interpret a world that she is in, yet ignored, pushed away, and left out of? I point out this little talked about taboo here because this kind of *Mama Trauma* is not something we usually expect to hear about and is a very significant insight into the multiple effects it has on parent-child and stepparent-stepchild relationships.

In the first place, it might be the underlying reason why a stepmother, who as a child was rejected by her own mother, is unable to emotionally connect with her stepchildren. Psychotherapists and perinatal psychologists say that a mother's capacity, or non-capacity, to feel emotionally attached and empathetic towards her infant daughter, even while in the womb, will have a direct effect on a child's developing brain related to her later capacity to love her own children, let alone someone else's.[2]

Secondly, in the case of the stepchild, this initial rejection, emotional detachment, and lack of love from their biological mother may be hindering the child's capacity for receiving love and acceptance from their stepmother. Thus, stepchild rejection of their stepparent's care may in fact be due to their early childhood rejection by their own biological mothers that the stepmother has inherited (probably unknowingly) and must now deal with daily. Not an easy task that only adds to the common cycle of tension in stepmother and stepchild relationships.

Emotional triangles are a common occurrence in all relationships. Simply put, they describe what can become an unhealthy three-person relationship. It suggests that there really is no such thing as a two-person relationship because everyone is connected to relationships with other people that ultimately influence the two-person relationship. For example, one can imagine the intensity of pressure created in a triangulated scenario between dad, child, and stepmom. If the stepmother is emotionally insecure and immature, she will cause a lot of tension between herself and stepchild forcing the dad to either take sides, or the dad will try to take responsibility for the child and stepmom's relationship, which causes more tension and unhealthy relationships between all three people (See Chapter Seven).

With the above insights, perhaps you realize more clearly that the tension you are having with your children or stepchildren is because you were a victim of rejection by your mother or stepmother. Understood. But there is hope.

This brings me back *to the myth of mother love* I shared at the beginning of this chapter, which I think is easier understood, sort of expected, and accepted in the case of stepmothers. As a stepmother, though not ideal, there is not the same amount of pressure and criticism that a biological mother receives who simply does not have the emotional connection, attachment, or love that is expected towards her newborn. Streep says, according to the expectations, pressure, and mores of Western culture, for a mother to admit this lack of love is to admit to the greatest failure as a woman and a person. Nevertheless, that is the reality for many mothers and the bold and controversial topic Streep addresses in her book. I applaud her for taking on this issue and highly recommend the book to any mother or stepmother who has experienced this kind of Mama Trauma with their mother or stepmother.

For our purposes here regarding Mama Trauma, if, as a stepmother you're having a lack of emotional connection with your stepchildren, it's understandable. However, the good news is that your love and connection can grow, and hopefully, you have the desire to make that happen. The key to this growth is the effort you make within yourself and not on the outward behavior of your stepchildren, although that does make it more challenging to be motivated to work on yourself. The initial rejection and cold-heartedness you may experience is painful, no doubt (I know it well myself). But that doesn't mean it can't change. It will also help with time and consistency of growth in emotional maturity, and integrity, and build bridges of trust.

For others who have suffered as a child with your stepparent and now you are a stepparent, the good news is there are those stepchildren who were neglected, abandoned, and severely abused, but endured and managed to overcome the Mama Trauma they experienced as told by Donna Ford in her book, *The Step Child: A True Story of a Broken Childhood*.[3]

Because of the brutal treatment and explosive hatred she received hourly and daily from her stepmother, Donna believed what any eight-year-old girl would believe about herself: that she was ugly, bad, and deserved her punishment. She was abandoned by her mother at the age of four, spent two years in a foster home, and then released to her father and stepmom only to be beaten, starved, ignored, and humiliated from day one, and never knowing the reason she was being punished.

Her punishment, amongst the beatings and starvation, included stripping down to her underwear and being made to stand in one spot in the bathroom from morning until bedtime. Or right after she got home from school until bedtime with no dinner. She was not allowed to sit or lie down or move from that one spot and not allowed to use the toilet. If she did, she would receive another beating. If she had to urinate, and asked to use the toilet, she would receive another beating and therefore would have to urinate on herself. But at least the warm urine, she said, would give her a bit of relief from her freezing legs and toes, until the urine itself grew cold. She was not allowed to shower or change her underwear when it was time to go to bed. In the morning, she was not allowed to change underwear and made to go to school smelling like urine. All the kids in her classroom ridiculed her and no one could stand to sit next to her because of the smell from her clothes. Kicked and used as a daily punching bag, bruises all over and bones sticking out, she wonders how nobody, not her teachers, family, or social workers that came to check up on and interview her, or even her father, ever noticed (which I have a hard time believing), said anything, asked anything, or did anything for a girl who was obviously being severely abused. Then, as she got a little older in her pre-teen years, the sexual abuse started with the friends of her stepmother who came to the house for the daytime parties her stepmom would have while her father was away at work.

I could go on, but I'm sure you get the picture. However, the amazing end of the story is that Donna grew up to be a caring, nurturing, and loving mother of her own children. She wrote her book because she wanted to stop being invisible. She wanted to share her story and be a voice of hope for other children of abuse to let them know that they too can overcome the traumatic life they've lived and to know they can have a future life of love and acceptance.

Donna's story is tragic. But I wanted to share it to illustrate that this particular kind of Mama Trauma (a stepmom in this case) can be overcome.

I've known stepparents who are good people. But they beat themselves up because their stepchild is rebellious, deviant, defiant, always in trouble, or, even worse, becomes a perpetrator of a crime and community violence. As one can imagine, this is a sad and hard road to travel. But, if this is your situation as you are reading this book, I encourage you not to give up on your stepchild. Do not give up this battle. And furthermore, do not give up on yourself to win this battle. As I mentioned earlier, the child you are struggling with may have hurts and wounds of rejection that have nothing to do with you. I know the difficulty of trying to build a relationship with one or both hands tied behind your back, so to speak. But you can succeed over time. If you find that you are part of the problem and are mature enough to admit it (I've been there too), that too can be overcome if you are willing to take responsibility. I will address this in later chapters in Part Two of this book and provide you with some tools to practice your personal growth skills in this area of relationship.

Rejection by Children Is a False Front

During my past career as a juvenile hall teacher and a correctional officer in two prisons, I witnessed even the toughest individuals break down in tears. Why? Because beneath their hardened exteriors, they felt unloved, unwanted, guilty, and rejected—by family, friends, and society.

What I learned from this was profound: though they acted as if they didn't care—about themselves or anyone else—it was all a façade. Deep down, they did care. They longed to be loved and accepted. They wanted to belong. And more than mere tolerance, they craved genuine embrace, despite their mistakes. Even if they couldn't put it into words, what they truly sought was unconditional love.

I believe every child inherently wants to do the right thing even when they know they are doing the wrong thing. However (as I've already mentioned), for a stepparent to not negatively react to the rejection requires us to be willing to do the inner work of emotional growth and stability within ourselves on a consistent basis. Admittedly, it's not easy with your own biological kids, let alone your stepchildren. However, I find that too many parents focus their efforts on trying to change the behavior of the child, rather than focusing on their own behavior that may be contributing to the defiant behavior. Transformation and reconciliation are possible long-term outcomes. NOT by trying to force change in the kids, but rather by focusing on our own personal growth. However, many stepparents are full of guilt, lack confidence, or are simply worn out emotionally and give in and give up since *it's not my kid anyway.*

This is understandable and goes back to what I said in the last chapter: how can a mother or stepmother actually mother stepchildren when she herself was not loved by her mother? Yet, the fact is they can . . . you can. If the desire is there. If you choose to take 100 percent responsibility for your life. If you choose not to be a victim of your past any longer and have the courage to address your own hurts, old wounds, and experience a breakthrough. You will overcome the past; you'll be free to receive and give the love needed. In his book, *A Failure of Nerve, Leadership in the Age of the Quick Fix,* Dr. Edwin H. Friedman speaks to the power of how just one parent with the willingness to take responsibility for their own personal growth, rather than placing blame on others in the family for the family dysfunction, can eventually be the sole change agent in a dysfunctional family.[4]

This what I call the *POM Experience* and what my Parents on a Mission Curriculum (I will share in Part Two) provides you with the tools to do so. I want any stepparent reading this book that may have suffered rejection from your own mother, or a similar (or worse) childhood as Donna Ford, to know it wasn't their fault. You can be healed, overcome, and give the love your stepchildren want, need, and deserve.

Single Parents Beware

A final and important point I want to make to single mothers and fathers: The Donna Ford story is only one of a plethora of voices of stepchildren in books, magazines, YouTube, Facebook, Instagram, and internet articles (Not to mention those I heard personally as a school at-risk counselor). Many stepchildren are filled with anger and hatred for their stepparents and stepsiblings.

Knowing this, single parents should listen to why these children are filled with anger and resentment and *hear* their testimonies of emotional, physical and psychological abuse, rape, and pedophilia. Their voice provides a *cautionary tale* that all single parents should give serious heed to, and very carefully consider who you allow to get close to your children and fulfill such a crucial role as stepparent in the life of your young children.

Key Takeaways for Chapter Four

- Stepparents and biological parents may bring unresolved emotional baggage into blended families, impacting relationships.
- Some children struggle with attachment issues due to past trauma or inconsistent parental relationships.
- Healing from past experiences and fostering a culture of trust is essential for a stable family environment.
- The role of forgiveness plays a major part in strengthening relationships within blended families.
- Open communication and emotional vulnerability help build authentic bonds between stepparents and stepchildren.

Action Plan for Chapter Four

- **Acknowledge Past Experiences:** Reflect on how past relationships impact your role as a stepparent.
- **Practice Forgiveness:** Let go of past grievances and model healthy emotional responses for children.
- **Seek Support When Needed:** Consider professional guidance, support groups, or family counseling to address persistent challenges.

CHAPTER FIVE
Death. Divorce. Hope.

Mama Trauma is a serious reality that can be experienced in several ways as I discussed above. The neglect, physical abuse, and emotional abuse is always hard to hear, but important to hear, nonetheless.

In addition to the kind of Mama Trauma I addressed in the previous chapter, I want to address another form of Mama Trauma—one that stems from loss, whether through death or divorce. But before I go any further, let me pause to acknowledge something important: my intention is not to burden you with sadness or sorrow by discussing these difficult topics.

I understand that revisiting painful experiences, especially those that were psychologically and emotionally challenging, can stir up emotions we might prefer to avoid, and that's completely understandable.

However, my ultimate goal is to bring hope. While loss is always painful, I want to assure you that hope is always present, too.

These circumstances are far from ideal. Divorce and unexpected loss are deeply tragic, often leaving us in an unfamiliar and disorienting state of mind. For stepparents and blended families, the journey may not begin on a joyful note, but rather from a place of pain caused by these life-altering events.

However, despite the challenges, healing is possible. These difficulties can be overcome. There is hope—and that is what I aim to demonstrate.

Earlier, I shared part of our blended family's journey—the challenges we've faced and the ongoing work to overcome them together. Now, I want to share a bit more about how our blended family came to be.

This isn't meant to recount every detail of our story, but rather to encourage those of you who have experienced, or are currently navigating, similar circumstances. If you've ever wondered whether things can truly get better, let me assure you—they can.

Death

It's four o'clock in the morning and the time has come to wake up my children. It was quiet, dark, and yet we had nowhere to be. Nowhere to go. Why then wake them up?

I was hanging on to the hope that I wouldn't need to wake them at such an hour. But that would require a miracle. A miracle that never came. The time had come. The fight was over. Their mom had lost her battle with breast cancer.

Perhaps I should have waited until they woke up later in the morning. But is there really a *right way* to go about this? Is there a better time to tell your children that their mother has passed away? Is there another way to complete their already broken hearts? I don't know. It was a new, unwanted territory for us all.

In December of 1993, we were enjoying another wonderful family vacation over the Christmas holiday in Big Bear, California. Snow, bobsleds, inner tube tires, snowmobile bikes, and most fun of all, playing Monopoly as a family. It had become our family tradition for Christmas and New Year's Eve. We would open Christmas presents on Christmas morning, then pack the van with our clothes, food, and kids' favorite toys and gifts, and then drive up to Big Bear for the week. But this time ended differently.

Towards the end of our vacation, my wife mentioned to me that she was feeling a slight pain from a very small lump in her breast. She wasn't overly concerned but mentioned it and then planned to go to the doctor for a checkup. While at the doctor's office they, of course, recommended a biopsy. Once that was completed all we could do was wait and see what the results would be. A very trying and worrisome wait.

I don't recall the exact time when the phone on the wall rang. But I do remember that each time it rang we would look at each other and wonder if it was *the call*. This time it was. On January 5, 1994, the bad news was delivered. She hung up the phone. The tears flowed. And our life was bitterly interrupted by that dreaded word: cancer.

After the call was received in January, little did we know that only ten short months later, on November 5, 1994, mama would be gone from here and from us.

At the time, my children were young. My boys were nineteen and fifteen. My girls were twelve, ten, and eight. To describe the emotionally shattered and distraught aftermath of my kids upon her passing is a Mama Trauma of a whole other kind and consequently set us on a whole other, unexpected path.

People say that time heals all pain, wounds, and all manner of hard and tragic circumstances. But my children will tell you that it doesn't. Not really. What time offers is learning how to cope with, live with, and deal with the pain of a certain hole in your heart that nothing else can fill. Memories are good. But they can also be painful. Simple things like birthdays, Mother's Day, Christmas, and special songs and places. Thus, a different kind and to a different degree, but Mama Trauma, nonetheless.

From the spouse's (or partner's) perspective, the trauma caused by either death or divorce puts you in the awkward position of being single again. Single, but not alone. Death is an uninvited intruder, yet one you can't make leave. Your world as you knew it comes to a stop. I remember how offended I was the day after my wife's funeral as I woke up. The sun still came up. The birds still sang. Neighbors got in their cars and drove to work and other kids still went to school. They didn't care that my world had stopped. Life, as it were, just kept on moving forward. It was a terrible realization. A side of the grave I had never been on. Suddenly, I had a perception and depth of knowledge and understanding of finality I did not want.

As the months went by, I could see how losing their mother was affecting my children, and ultimately their pain and need became my focus that helped me through my own pain and darkness even though I wasn't exactly sure what to do or how to handle their trauma. I decided to try and do something to fix everything . . . but I moved too fast, which ultimately only added to their Mama Trauma.

Divorce

Single again. Five kids. Full-time work. All good excuses to hurry up the process of finding a helpmate for myself. But it was all too fast. Too much. Too soon. And too bad. My bad.

I never stopped to consider or ask my kids for their thoughts. I didn't seek advice from others who may have gone through a similar circumstance that could have shed light on what it might mean for my kids to remarry too soon. I didn't allow us to get help with a long-term grieving process that would have been better for us all . . . I just plowed full steam ahead and remarried. It didn't last a year. And no fault of hers. It was all me that caused the divorce.

The divorce fell right into the statistical category of a failed remarriage. But the worst part, and the point I'm making here, was the added Mama Trauma for my children losing another mother not so long after losing their biological mother. And that is the sad fate of so many children who lose their mother or stepmother by death, divorce, or separation. In the case of divorce, remarriage, and divorce again, the children suffer . . . again and again. We cause them to become innocent victims through these life-changing decisions they had nothing to do with and oftentimes don't overcome. Some grow up to become a menace to society and/or go on to become parents themselves and repeat the cycle of divorce or separation from their own and someone else's children causing even more innocent suffering. I'm not saying this happens one hundred percent of the time, but the statistics I mentioned at the beginning of this book speak for themselves. However, there is hope.

Hope

It grieves me when I think about the Mama Trauma my children have been through. Looking back, it has been a long, drawn-out series of emotional stress. Ups and downs. Disappointments, failures, heartache, pain, arguments, hurts, and a whole lot of tears. But, over the years, combined with a progression of joy, laughter, love, faith in God, forgiveness, and still a whole lot of tears, we have made great progress as a healthy, happy blended family.

Our current blended family, the Ramos/Gonzalez/Ramirez family (as of 2002), as mentioned earlier, did not come together in the best of circumstances. We came together under negative circumstances. However, my desire in sharing our story is to provide you with hope. The hope for you stepparents reading this book. The hope that comes with patience, integrity, consistency, forgiveness, and unconditional love. The hope for single parents to believe they will bring the right person into the lives of their children. A soul mate who will love them and whom they will love. The hope for married stepparents that your blended family can get better. And though you may have incurred many obstacles, I pray our story will inspire the hope and faith to believe things can get better and your challenges can be overcome.

The current relationship that my children have with my wife, and that her children have with me, is the result of overcoming many such obstacles. But today, and for many years now, it is and has been wonderful. Our children constantly and continually express their love at every opportunity that presents itself: Mother's Day, Father's Day, Birthdays, Christmas, Easter, Thanksgiving, Holidays, family outings, parties, vacations together. It is so great and satisfying to enjoy our blended family. We often make time to simply hang out with as many of our children, grandchildren, and now three great-grandchildren (new additions to our family as of this writing) to laugh and enjoy each other's company. There is nothing that brings us more joy.

In closing, it is true that my wife and I have our regrets. But we took full responsibility for the choices we made. And we accept that our choices caused hurt for our children, family, friends, and ourselves. But through unconditional love, faith, forgiveness, and personal growth in emotional maturity, we have endured. My message of hope to you is that, though we still face challenges, we are happy. We are together. And we are here to provide stepparents reading this book, facing and enduring similar challenges, with the inspiration and encouragement that you can do it too!

Key Takeaways for Death and Divorce in Mama Trauma

- **Loss impacts children deeply:** The death of a parent or divorce can create feelings of abandonment, grief, and insecurity in children, shaping their emotional responses to relationships.
- **Unresolved grief affects behavior:** Children who do not process their emotions from loss may develop behavioral issues, withdrawal, or difficulty forming new bonds.
- **Stepparents must navigate grief sensitively:** It is important to acknowledge the child's pain and not attempt to replace their biological parent but rather offer support and consistency.
- **Divorce can create divided loyalties:** Children may struggle with feeling disloyal to one parent if they bond with a stepparent, requiring patience and reassurance.
- **Healing takes time and effort:** Encouraging open discussions about emotions, providing stability, and fostering a sense of security can help children process their experiences in a healthy way.

Action Plan for Addressing Death and Divorce in Mama Trauma

1. **Create Safe Spaces for Grieving**
   - Allow children to express their emotions freely without judgment.
   - Validate their pain and reassure them that their feelings are normal.

2. **Avoid Forcing Relationships**
   - Allow children to bond with a stepparent at their own pace.
   - Respect the child's need for space while continuing to offer support.

3. **Support Their Relationship with the Biological Parent**
   - Encourage ongoing connections with the biological parent whenever possible.
   - Be mindful of not speaking negatively about the ex-spouse or deceased parent.

4. **Seek Professional Support When Needed**
   - Encourage therapy or counseling if a child struggles to process their emotions.
   - Consider family counseling to navigate the complexities of loss and blended family dynamics.

CHAPTER SIX
The Stepdad Gap

I remember a moment when my three oldest kids had become teenagers, and I found myself needing to apologize for some mistakes I had made as their father. I was in a period of personal growth and had begun to see how it was impacting them. They were starting to notice—and resent—that their two younger siblings were benefiting from a more patient, understanding, and flexible version of me. Recognizing this, I decided to sit down with them and share my heart. I wanted to apologize for the experiences they had with a younger, less experienced father.

I wasn't abusive, but I had been overly strict and intolerant in ways that I knew might have hurt them emotionally. As I addressed each of them, I turned to my oldest son—my stepson, whom I had raised since he was two—and apologized for being too harsh in disciplining him at times. To my surprise, he broke down and began to cry. Until that moment, I hadn't realized how deeply I had hurt him, nor how long he had been carrying that pain in his heart. It was a powerful and humbling moment. I could feel and see that healing was taking place between us.

All that was left to do was to embrace him, cry together, and sincerely apologize. Up to that point, we had a good relationship, but from that moment on, it deepened in ways I hadn't expected. Our bond grew stronger, and it remains so to this day.

But what I want to address here is the question of why? Why did I discipline him too harshly in the first place? Why had I acted that way?

The honest answer is that he wasn't my biological son. It wasn't that I didn't care for him or have a love for him—I did. But at that point in my life, I had to confront the reality that I wasn't being the best version of myself as a dad or a stepdad.

Recognizing this harshness and favoritism towards biological children, or however else this imbalance might manifest, is an essential step if we want to change it and close what I call the "Stepdad Gap." The growth into a more equal, loving, and healthy relationship with our stepchildren requires self-awareness and emotional maturity. This kind of growth doesn't happen automatically—it takes intentional internal work, which I will discuss in later chapters.

This realization often brings guilt because our conscience confronts us with the truth about our harshness, intolerance, unfairness, or lack of emotional attachment. But guilt, while uncomfortable, can be a catalyst for transformation if we're willing to face it and put in the effort. Unfortunately, this is where many stepdads fall short.

It's easy to ignore the voice of conscience, dismiss the

conviction we feel, or justify our behavior rather than do the hard work of growth and self-improvement. Immaturity, pride, or simply not knowing how to be different from the way we were raised often stands in the way. Some stepdads may not see the value in changing or lack the motivation to address the strain that exists in their relationships.

But building a better relationship—a bond that bridges the Stepdad Gap—requires breaking those cycles. It demands humility, emotional growth, and the willingness to put effort into closing the distance between stepdads and stepchildren. When we do this, we create relationships rooted in love, respect, and connection.

Kyle Robinson shares a powerful and painful account of his stepdad in his story, *What It's Like to Be Abused by the Man Your Mom Wants You to Call Dad.*[1] He describes the physical and verbal abuse he endured from the moment his stepdad entered his life. As Kyle grew older, the abuse shifted from physical to primarily verbal, with his stepdad frequently calling him a loser and using insults designed to belittle, embarrass, and shame him. Despite this, Kyle reveals at the end of his story that his stepdad, whom he nicknamed "Triple B" (short for Big Bad Ben), was himself a victim of child abuse. Because of this, Kyle believed his stepdad was incapable of being anything other than abusive—a tragic cycle of pain that had passed down through generations.

Beyond the physical and verbal abuse that Kyle shared in his story, there is the devastating reality of sexual abuse by stepdads, a horrific violation that is tragically common in many stories shared by young girls and women. It is a tragedy of the worst kind, a profound betrayal, and an unspeakable trauma no child should ever have to endure. Unfortunately, it is a grim reality that single mothers must be vigilant about, as I highlighted in an earlier chapter. This issue serves as a stark reminder of the need for awareness, caution, and protection to break the cycles of harm and create safe environments for children.

Closing the Stepdad Gap

A crucial first step in closing this gap is simply acknowledging that it exists. This requires nothing more than being honest with yourself. If you find yourself struggling to feel a natural connection with your stepchildren, it's important not to let guilt overwhelm you. Initial awkwardness in these situations is normal and understandable. It's similar to the discomfort you might feel when meeting anyone new—whether it's future in-laws, colleagues, a blind date, your friend's friends, or new classmates. The difference, of course, is that in this case, you're married to the child's mother, and now you all live together. This shared environment requires a deeper level of adjustment, which can be challenging but necessary for everyone involved.

The real work begins when you commit to making those adjustments across several areas of your role as a stepdad. It's not always easy, but it's in these efforts that meaningful relationships can begin to grow, and the emotional gap can start to close. These roles include:

1. **A Position of Authority**: This can vary greatly depending on your relationship with your spouse and

the dynamics of who takes the lead in the household. In some cases, you may hold a position of authority, while in others, you may take a backseat depending on who wears the proverbial pants in the family.

2. **Disciplinarian**: Whether or not you take on the role of disciplinarian often depends on how your spouse feels about your style of discipline and involvement in setting and enforcing rules. Some mothers may prefer to handle discipline themselves, while others may expect you to share this responsibility.

3. **Provider**: Acting as the family provider can also become a source of tension, depending on how you and your spouse view work, money, and family finances. Aligning these issues is crucial to avoiding misunderstandings or resentment.

4. **Family Reconciler and Peacemaker**: This role demands significant emotional maturity, especially when conflicts arise. Whether the tension is between stepsiblings, between the mother and her children, or even between you and your stepchildren, navigating these dynamics requires patience, understanding, and a commitment to fostering harmony.

I may be leaving out other scenarios, but by now, the point is clear. These challenges can emerge suddenly and intensely or persist as an ongoing reality in a blended family. Over time, they can lead to burnout, disengagement, or even the choice to walk away entirely.

This avoidance creates the *Stepdad Gap*—the decision to withdraw from the responsibilities and consequences that come with blending families.

I've personally witnessed this dynamic among family, friends, and clients. As someone who has chosen to step up rather than step out, I fully understand the hardships these situations present. I also understand why some—perhaps many—stepdads struggle to step up, which only widens the Stepdad Gap.

The emotional ups and downs of a blended family can be both exhilarating and exhausting. There are stretches—days, weeks, even months—when everything seems to be going smoothly. Relationships appear to be strengthening, and life feels like it's finally moving toward that vision of happiness and harmony you've been working toward. But then, something happens to remind you that things aren't as far along as you'd hoped.

Take the holidays, for example—Christmas, Thanksgiving, or a birthday celebration. Everyone seems happy, getting along, and enjoying the occasion. Relationships with each other's kids appear to be improving, and on the surface, it feels like progress. Yet, there's often an intangible *strain* lingering in the air. No one says anything, but the body language and awkward conversations speak volumes. Or sometimes, someone does something or *says* something like a careless comment about an unresolved grievance. Maybe someone drinks too much, feels overwhelmed, or struggles with the situation and either leaves abruptly or doesn't show up at all. It's like a delicate dance: two steps forward, three steps back. And the pattern repeats, back and forth, over the years.

So, you ask yourself, *has there been growth? Have things improved? Has our blended family truly blended? Are we in a better place today than we were before?* The answer is hard to know sometimes. Nevertheless, if we continue to put in the work, though progress may be slow and uneven, it will be there, and it's worth celebrating. The key is to recognize it's about me working on *myself*, not on the kids. I tried that approach, focusing on them, but it didn't work. Sure, you might get outward compliance, but it does nothing to address the inward resentment and bitterness that can block a genuine, healthy relationship. No, the real key to closing the Stepdad Gap lies in personal growth and emotional maturity. It's about developing a well-defined sense of self that enables self-differentiation—an ability to maintain your individuality while allowing others in the family system to do the same.

This approach stands in stark contrast to the herd mentality, where everyone is guilt-tripped or forced into conformity, leaving little space for individual family members to find their own voice and path while staying connected to the new blended family. This principle applies to biological fathers in traditional families as well, but it's particularly important for stepdads who want to bridge the gap and create meaningful, lasting relationships.

Key Takeaways for Chapter Six

- Stepdads often struggle with balancing authority and building trust within blended families.
- Many stepdads feel pressure to establish their role quickly, which can lead to resistance from stepchildren.
- Earning respect as a stepdad takes time, consistency, and emotional intelligence. Open communication, empathy, and patience are essential to bridging the Stepdad Gap.

Action Plan for Chapter Six:

1. **Set Realistic Expectations:** Understand that building trust with stepchildren takes time and cannot be rushed.
2. **Establish Boundaries Together:** Work with your spouse to define clear roles and expectations for parenting.
3. **Focus on Relationship First:** Prioritize bonding activities over discipline to foster connection with stepchildren.
4. **Communicate Openly with Your Partner:** Ensure both biological and stepparenting roles are mutually respected.
5. **Remain Patient and Consistent:** Show up daily with patience, support, and consistency to gradually earn stepchildren's trust.

CHAPTER SEVEN
The Blended Family Triangle

In his book *The Failure of Nerve: Leadership in the Age of the Quick Fix,* Dr. Edwin H. Friedman explains that there is no such thing as a purely two-person relationship. This is because each of us is deeply connected to significant relationships within our family of origin, as well as various other relationships we've developed over time with extended family members, neighbors, close friends, teammates, college roommates, and others. These connections inevitably influence the so-called two-person relationship we believe exists in marriage. This dynamic, which I refer to as the "blended family triangle," is also commonly known as an emotional triangle.

Emotional triangles are a concept in psychology most closely associated with the work of Murray Bowen, known as family systems therapy.[1] Bowen theorized that a two-person emotional system is unstable; under stress, it forms itself into a three-person system or triangle. Triangles can have either negative or positive outcomes depending on how their members manage anxiety and reactivity. Triangulation can complicate relationships and perpetuate unhealthy dynamics.

Patterns in Triangles

The dynamics within a triangle change with increasing tension:

- **In Calm Periods:** Two people are *insiders* who are comfortably close, while the third person is an *outsider*, who feels excluded and works to regain closeness with one of the insiders.
- **Moderate Tension:** The most uncomfortable insider moves closer to the outsider. This reshapes the triangle, so the outsider becomes an insider, and the original insider now becomes the new outsider. The tension typically results in one conflicted side and two harmonious sides.
- **High Tension:** At high levels of tension, the outside position becomes the most desirable. If conflict between the insiders escalates, one insider may maneuver to shift the outsider into a fight with the other insider. The maneuvering insider gains the comfortable position of watching the other two fight.

The introduction of a third person (like a child, partner, or stepparent) may provide temporary relief from direct conflict, but the underlying issue remains unresolved. In stepfamilies, the stepparent starts as the outsider, which can lead to feelings of rejection and anxiety. Over time, they may attempt to bond more closely with the biological parent or the stepchild, creating shifting alliances. These dynamics can feel unpredictable and emotionally taxing for everyone involved. This can strain bonds and lead to long-term conflicts.

In addition, triangles in stepfamilies can form over issues of discipline, leniency, protectiveness, freedom, and individuality. Or it can form around various relationships within the blended family system.

For example, a single mom has a son. She decides to marry again. This is an automatic triangle situation and can either be good or bad depending on how the biological mother and stepdad react to tension caused by a child and/or children in any of the following scenarios.

Scenario one: The son speaks to his mother in a manner the stepdad perceives as disrespectful. Wanting to protect and support his wife, the stepdad steps in to correct the stepson for his behavior. In response, the stepson protests, arguing that the stepdad is not *his father* and therefore has no right to discipline him. The mother, siding with her son, creates tension in the marriage and reshapes the family triangle, leaving the stepdad in the outsider role.

Scenario two: The stepdad observes that his wife is overly critical and harsh toward her son. Having experienced a similar upbringing with his own mother, he empathizes with his stepson and decides to share his own experiences of estrangement from his mother as a result of similar treatment. However, his wife reacts with anger, feels offended, and argues with him. The stepdad, feeling protective of his stepson, takes the boy's side, which reshapes the family triangle, leaving the mother as the new outsider.

Scenario three: A couple, each with children from previous relationships, decides to marry and blend their families. Over time, conflicts arise between the stepsiblings, who begin complaining to their respective parents. Each parent sides with their own children, creating conflicting triangles, escalating tension and anxiety within the marriage while also perpetuating ongoing conflict among the stepsiblings.

Scenario four: In this scenario, a single mother with one daughter marries a man with three daughters. The stepdaughters are mean and abusive toward their youngest stepsister. When the youngest daughter complains to her mother, the mother—eager to gain the approval of her new husband and stepdaughters—sides with the stepdaughters, dismissing her own daughter's claims as lies. This dynamic leaves the daughter feeling excluded and positions her as the outsider within the blended family triangle.

When these triangle conflicts arise in stepfamily dynamics, stepparents should first take an honest look at their own role in the situation. This reflection isn't about assigning blame but about recognizing the influence they have as additional caregivers. The key to handling these situations and to avoid becoming triangulated is for parents to avoid taking sides and instead listen to all perspectives while maintaining relationships with everyone involved. Rather than trying to fix the situation by forcing the other parties to resolve their differences, it's more effective to foster open communication. Taking sole responsibility for complex relationships can add unnecessary stress to stepparents and further complicate family dynamics.

Positive Steps for Stepfamilies

Reflection, Not Blame: Stepparents are encouraged to reflect on their role in the family system without assigning or internalizing blame. This helps reduce tension in triangles and fosters healthier dynamics.

Recognition of Stepparent Roles: Stepmothers, in particular, are highlighted as significant figures in a child's life. Their contributions should be recognized and valued, not overshadowed by comparisons to the biological parent.

Avoiding Overfocus on a Child: It is crucial to avoid making a child the focus of family tension. When parents or stepparents unintentionally triangulate a child into their conflicts, it can lead to long-term emotional challenges for the child.

Breaking the Cycle: To prevent triangles from becoming destructive, all members of the family must learn to manage their own anxiety and avoid triangulating others. This involves:

1. Open communication between stepparents and biological parents (if possible).
2. Setting boundaries to ensure children are not pulled into adult conflicts.
3. Developing self-awareness to recognize when one is perpetuating unhealthy dynamics.
4. Build Authentic Relationships: Stepparents should work towards building authentic relationships and

not try to replace a biological parent. The focus is to create a supportive, respectful, and trustworthy relationship.

Emotional triangles, while a natural part of human relationships, can create significant challenges in stepfamilies. By recognizing and addressing these patterns, stepparents can create healthier dynamics that support all members.

To effectively embrace the important and challenging role of stepparents, it is essential to take responsibility for our personal growth in emotional maturity. This growth empowers us to navigate the complexities of our position with self-awareness and compassion, a focus that is explored in the next and final section of this book.

Key Takeaways for Chapter Seven: The Blended Family Triangle

- Emotional triangles are common in blended families and can create tension between parents, stepparents, and children.
- Understanding these dynamics helps prevent manipulation and favoritism from shaping family interactions.
- Biological parents play a crucial role in mediating relationships and ensuring fair treatment for all children.
- Establishing clear roles and expectations helps prevent misunderstandings and conflict within the family structure.

Action Plan for Chapter Seven

1. **Identify Existing Triangles:** Recognize where emotional triangles are forming and address them openly.
2. **Communicate Directly:** Encourage direct conversations between stepparents and stepchildren rather than relying on the biological parent as a go-between.
3. **Encourage Family Bonding:** Create activities that involve all members to foster unity and minimize division.
4. **Address Issues Early:** Do not ignore signs of tension; use family meetings or counseling to resolve conflicts before they escalate.

PART TWO

POM PRINCIPLES AND THE STEPPARENT'S ROLE AS A TRANSFORMATIONAL LEADER

Parents on a Mission is not just a book or a program; it's a movement. It is a bold, inspiring call to action for parents, stepparents, single parents, foster parents, and caregivers of children to step into their role as transformational leaders in their homes and communities. Its focus on self-growth, emotional maturity, and reconciliation provides a holistic framework that extends far beyond traditional parenting advice. It empowers readers to reclaim their influence and to rethink their role in shaping the next generation. Its practical steps make it a valuable resource for anyone seeking to raise emotionally healthy, responsible, and resilient children.

While this book focuses on *The Art of Stepparenting*, the POM principles presented here are the same as those featured in my POM curriculum and book. However, some of the principles have been adapted slightly to address the unique challenges and dynamics of stepparents, stepchildren, and blended families.

CHAPTER EIGHT
The POM Medal of Honor–Recognizing Your Worth as a Stepparent

Our society does a fair job of recognizing and promoting as heroes and role models sports stars, rock stars, and movie stars. Recognition is also given to people in positions of social status, like teachers, policemen, politicians, and the like. I'm not suggesting that these individuals don't deserve recognition for their accomplishments and contributions. But what I am saying is that parents who do so much for their children in service and sacrifice deserve as much, if not more, recognition from society than they are usually given. And this same recognition applies to stepparents as well, who are willing to deal with all the challenges discussed in Part One of this book (plus other challenges I did not cover). Consequently, I've discovered that parents don't perceive themselves as significant players in their community the way they should. When I ask parents who they consider to be the most important people in the community, the answer is usually not parents, but rather others like pastors, priests, principals of schools, politicians, etc. Again, I'm not suggesting these individuals don't deserve credit and recognition for the services they provide to the community. Yet, in my mind, and what I continue to emphasize to moms and dads nurturing families, is that they are the most important assets in the community more than any other single individual or entity when it comes to producing safe and healthy communities.

Think about it. Where do the citizens of the community come from? Citizens go to church. They don't come from church. They go to school. They don't come from school. Citizens go to work and public places of service. They don't come from there. They're not produced and raised there. The fact is citizens of the community come from our homes. And the question is: What kind of citizens are we sending out to the community every day? But I'm getting ahead of myself and will address that subject in a later chapter.

Let's get back to the POM Medal of Honor. For this exercise, parents are provided a simple graphic that has four quadrants where they are asked to write the following:

- Quadrant One: Write three positive words that describe you (Or how you think your children/stepchildren would positively describe you).
- Quadrant Two: Choose one word that best describes your greatest strength as a person and/or a stepparent.
- Quadrant Three: List the services you provide your children/stepchildren on a regular basis.
- Quadrant Four: List the sacrifices you have made

(or would be willing to make) for your children/stepchildren.

I invite you to stop reading for a moment and do this seemingly simple exercise yourself and see how it goes.

Instructions

Get a sheet of regular 8.5" X 11" paper. Draw a vertical line down the middle of the paper. Next, divide the square into four separate quadrants by drawing a horizontal line across the middle of the paper intersecting with the vertical line and thus giving you four separate quadrants/spaces to write in. Now, answer the four different questions above in each quadrant.

What is always amazing to me is how parents struggle with this exercise, especially with the first two quadrants. Why? When we discuss this, it comes down to a self-esteem issue or lack thereof. They don't know how to speak well of or positively honor themselves. They are at a loss for how to describe themselves in a *great way*. They have never been asked to do such a thing. For some, it is almost an anathema to speak of oneself this way; it's bragging, bigheaded, narcissistic, and *not okay*.

To give a little encouragement, I usually give some examples to get them going in the spirit of the exercise. For example, I'll write in the first quadrant that I am generous, humorous, and understanding. In quadrant two, I'll write *understanding* and explain that I believe my children would agree with me that I am an understanding father, etc. These examples usually helps them—and gives them permission—to speak of themselves this way and then we are off, and running.

Once all have had a little more time to work on their medal of honor, I ask for volunteers to come in front of the class and share their medal of honor with the rest of us. However, I don't just let them come up and read the words. I probe and ask them to explain why they wrote what they wrote.

This simple exercise is so powerful. It is truly an amazing process to watch many get emotional, even breakdown, while others swell in a healthy pride, being affirmed by the group that they are, in fact, important, significant, and a crucial part of developing the community because of the influence they are having at home with their children. They begin *to see* themselves differently. They begin to accept that they, like others given community recognition and honor, deserve it as well.

CHAPTER NINE
Personal Growth for Stepparents- Managing Emotions and Expectations

I have created a simple four-step process to practice (on an ongoing basis) the principles for personal growth in emotional maturity.

A. The Process of Self Examination–Know *yourself to grow yourself*

- Get into a habit (discipline) of making time daily to slow down, get quiet, and think, meditate, and/or pray.
- During this time (maybe ten minutes or more), practice listening to your heart and conscience. Grow in your sensitivity to that small voice within.
- Practice thinking about your thinking about yourself. In other words, pay attention to your thoughts about you.
- Finally, when around others, pay attention to your self-talk. This is one of the best ways to discover your

thoughts about yourself. The words you say out loud about yourself are revealing. Are they negative, put-downs, self-doubting?

Self-examination requires a willingness to acknowledge my strengths and weaknesses, my moods and emotional inconsistencies, my likes and dislikes, my priorities and prejudices, and a reaffirmation of my values. In other words, we need to be authentic.

Why is all this important? It's important because all our relationships with others flow out of our relationship with ourselves.

Signs of Growth in Emotional Maturity

How can I know when I'm growing? What are some indicators I can look for to measure my progress? The following is not a comprehensive list, but it does give some simple metrics we can easily be aware of.

I know I am making progress in my emotional maturity when:

- I find I have more self-control under stressful situations.
- Others (like my children) acknowledge that I am more patient than they know me to be.
- I am more cooperative at work, home, school. Even when I don't get my way, I still cooperate as a good team player.
- I am not as quick to speak my mind. I am more

considerate about how my words, comments, and opinions might negatively affect others.
- I am not as rigid in my attitude. I am much more flexible in my thinking and receiving new ideas or ways of doing things.
- I am willing to acknowledge my mistakes and apologize without making excuses.
- I am more in control of my anger. I am learning to use it for the right reason, towards the right person, in the right place, at the right time, and to the right degree.

The process of learning to know myself, while rewarding, can also uncover and shed light on things that are uncomfortable. It often exposes the fact that we have a negative self-image that seems so embedded and difficult, if not impossible, to change. The bad news is we have cultivated faulty thoughts that have caused a negative self-image. The good news is our thought-life can be brought under our control and therefore we are empowered to change and transform the negative into a positive self-image. Here's one example:

> *Richard, I must say my way of thinking and approach to life and parenting has been forever changed by the recent POM training I received . . . on a personal level, I have been able to see where I went wrong [and] made amends with my daughter and myself. I stopped blaming myself and simply named myself as the parent God created me to be. Thank you so much for this gift. It has taken me a*

> *long time to overcome my shame.*
> –Rhonda Starr, Bakersfield, CA

B. Know the Power of My Thoughts

Oftentimes, we wonder why we do or say certain hurtful things to those we love. To help discover answers to that question I encourage parents in this next step to be honest and willing to go deep in their hearts. This is a process that could lead to discovering answers to bring healing to unresolved wounds, shame, guilt, or resentment from our past that have not been dealt with and are at the root of unhealthy relationships with our children. Author and leadership expert John Maxwell says that hurting people often hurt people and are easily hurt by them. That is a very telling statement that provides the kind of insight we need to heal how we treat ourselves and others.

Admittedly, peeling back the layers of years to examine our thoughts about ourselves can be challenging. Yet, it can also be very liberating to discover reasons for why we think the way we do about ourselves and then understand that we can change our thinking as needed.

Here's another principle I use to help emphasize just how powerful our thoughts are: Sow a thought, reap an action. Sow an action, reap a habit. Sow a habit, reap a character. Sow a character, reap a destiny.

This little phrase is a simple but powerful formula for personal growth from the inside-out; the point being that *sowing* actions, habits, and character ultimately leads to our destiny, and it all begins with our thinking.

The fact is that sowing and reaping is a universal principle that works whether we understand it or not. But when we come to understand this principle, we have the power as human beings to use it to our benefit. In other words, we can control our destiny, change our current circumstances, and create a better life for our families, beginning with controlling our thoughts, mostly about ourselves.

How to Identify and Overcome Our Negative Thoughts and Self-Talk

Allow me to elaborate a little more on simple ways to identify the negative thoughts swirling around in our heads:

1. **Give more attention and focus on your inner conversation and/or reflections.** For example, you wake up early in the morning and, while lying in bed, your mind just starts racing about a job or project you need to finish. Where does your mind go?
   - Rather than being happy, confident, and excited because you know you're going to *crush it,* you begin to have thoughts of stress, anxiety, doubt, fear, etc.
   - You get a phone call offering you the opportunity you have worked for, hoped for, and said you wanted. But then you begin to wonder, *Can I really do this job? Is this really the best thing for me? Is this the right time to make this career change, and what will others think and say if I leave the security of my current job?*

2. **Listen to your self-talk and the words you use about you.** For example, when someone gives you a compliment, how do you respond?

- Wow, you really look great in that dress! But then you say, *Yeah, but it doesn't fit me right and I look funny in this color . . . don't I?*
- Hey, good job on your talk today! But then you say, *Thanks, but I forgot to mention some important points and then I got off course and took too long . . . didn't I?*
- Did you get a new haircut and color? It looks great! But then you say, *it's okay, but I don't like it as much as I thought I would, and the color is a little off . . . don't you think?*

If the above sounds familiar, join the negative self-talk club. But maybe you're thinking, *well, isn't that me just being humble?* I don't know. Is it? That's the thing we are learning here. What we might pass off for humility could be how we deceive ourselves and rationalize our habit of putting ourselves down and doubting ourselves. In that case, it's time to face the hard truth that we really have a problem with our self-image. And what I'm emphasizing here is the importance of exploring how that happens, and more importantly, what I can—and should—do about it?

Before I give you the answer of what to do about it and how to overcome this mind-set, let me back up a moment and remind us about why this is important regarding parenting. If we realize that we don't have the relationships we want with our children/stepchildren and we want that to change, that change must begin with ourselves. And as stepparents, we also understand that a solid, fun, healthy, and respectful relationship with our stepchildren does not always happen automatically. Thus, to *sow the seeds* and do the work to cultivate that healthy parent-child relationship, we need to acknowledge that all of our relationships flow out of our relationship with ourself. That's why this is important. That's why this inside-out process of emotional maturity is worth the work it takes to grow.

The growth exercise I'm sharing with you here to overcome negative thoughts may seem simple, but it is not easily mastered. It takes practice just like any new habit or skill. Nothing grows overnight. To overcome deeply embedded wounds of shame, guilt, self-loathing, fear, and other types of emotional hang-ups takes discipline and the courage not to give in when that negative voice tells you you're *wasting your time and will never change*. But, if you practice this simple exercise consistently, I promise you will experience personal growth and transformation.

Three steps to transformation from the inside-out:

You must become:
1. A thought catcher.
2. A thought changer.
3. A thought replacer.

There you have it. Sound simple? Well, it is relatively simple in theory, but not in practice at the beginning stages. Yet, anyone willing and wanting to change can do this and will experience growth in emotional maturity.

Let's go a little deeper into each of these steps:

- Catching our thoughts requires focus, attentiveness, practice, and self-awareness.
- Changing our negative thoughts to positive thoughts requires belief, discipline, and courage.
- Replacing our negative thoughts with positive thoughts requires verbal self-affirmation. These are *I am* statements spoken out loud, so we hear ourselves affirm ourselves in the positive. And writing them down and putting them somewhere using post it notes on your computer, refrigerator, bathroom mirror, etc. where you will see them and read them daily.

Some examples:

If I hear myself say to myself (either in my head or out loud), *I'll never lose all this extra weight, I'm a terrible mother, I'm not good enough, No one cares about me,* etc.

- I "catch" that thought because now I'm self-aware of my negative thinking and I now know I don't have to accept it. I can catch and control my thoughts.
- I change this negative thought to a positive thought in my mind first. I have an internal conversation with self . . . something like, *No. I'm not accepting that about me. I am a good person and a good mother.*
- I then say the positive self-affirming thought out loud to myself by making I am or I can statements such as *I am a good person and a good mother,* or something to that effect.

Talking to yourself this may seem awkward at first, but I assure you it is a very powerful method of *self-talk* that will change your life if you persist.

Dr. Nate Zinsser is a well-known performance psychology expert who has spent the last three decades teaching soldiers, professional athletes, and executives the principles of mental toughness. One of the techniques he teaches he calls "getting in the last word," meaning to pay attention to our internal negative thoughts, fears, and worries, and making sure we win the competition between these negative and positive competing voices by getting in the last word.

For you to win in those moments requires that you practice these three basic steps: 1) catch the negative thought, 2) change the negative thought, and 3) replace the negative thought with a positive affirmation.

The Power of Our Words

Remember the old saying, "Sticks and stones may break my bones, but words can never hurt me?" Nothing could be further from the truth. We all know how hurtful words can be. There's a verse in the Bible that says the power of death and life are in the tongue; in the words we speak. I believe that is the truth.

Some of you reading this book have been devastated by the words of a parent, relative, teacher, coach, or significant other. Words can be our greatest weapon to build up another or to tear them down.

One day, when I was a young boy, my dad asked me what I wanted to be when I grew up. At the time, I was probably about nine or ten years old. I was a huge Dodgers fan as we grew up ten minutes from Dodger Stadium in Los Angeles. My brother and I were pretty good athletes and played all the sports at the local park with other neighborhood kids. Baseball was my favorite sport, and being a left-handed pitcher, I modeled everything I did on the mound after my boyhood idol, Sandy Koufax, the great Hall of Fame pitcher for the Los Angeles Dodgers. So, when my dad asked me this question, I answered with the same aspirations that most young athletes have, which is to play in the big leagues. I said, ?I want to play for the Dodgers."

Now, think about the situation. Here I was, a young impressionable boy, standing there waiting for my dad to encourage, motivate, and affirm my aspirations as silly or as unrealistic as they might have been. But that's not what he did. He sarcastically said, "Huh? Who do you think you are? Do you really think you're good enough?"

Crushing! Those *words* shook me and haunted me for a long time.

I'm not saying my dad meant to emotionally crush me (I really don't know if he did or didn't). Nevertheless, it did affect my mind negatively, tore at my self-confidence, and contributed to my being a very self-conscious person. Of course, I never understood any of that as I grew up. I just intuitively knew I didn't have the confidence and faith in myself I needed as an athlete wanting to play professionally. But these words began to show up in other areas of my life and it took me years to overcome them, and I did it by practicing the very things I am sharing with you here.

With our words, we can move people to laughter or tears. With our words, we can motivate a whole nation with a "I have a dream" speech. By the words of a song, the words in a book, or the dialogue in a movie, we can capture the hearts and imagination of an audience both old and young alike.

So, why am I saying all this? Because I want you to realize why it's important for you to hear yourself say to yourself the positive affirmations in this exercise. Words are powerful! My words, their words, and your words. Therefore, use your own words to build yourself up on a consistent basis and do not give this power away to others when they try to bring you down, or when your own negative thoughts try to bring you down. Use your word weapon correctly and watch your life change.

C. Use Your Power of Choice

All of us have faced certain challenges in life that tend to overwhelm us emotionally and therefore steal our joy. We often allow these past and current circumstances to dictate our quality of life. We get caught up in what is commonly known as a *victim mentality*, meaning that we feel there is nothing we can do about our situation. *It is what it is*, as they say, and we embrace this idea that it's someone else's fault and/or someone else's responsibility to do something to change or improve my situation. We live in a *blame game* bubble, always looking outside ourselves for reasons why we are not happy, unsuccessful, overlooked, discriminated against, and basically a *victim of circumstances*.

To be fair, there certainly are people in power in this world who are not fair and do discriminate, and sometimes, in life, we can be in the wrong place at the wrong time. Nevertheless, the point I'm getting at here is we don't have to accept our circumstances as unchangeable or as something we can't take responsibility for, and we can decide to change the situation. One such person who is a great example of facing the most difficult of circumstances and deciding not to be *overcome by events* is Mrs. Rose Kennedy.

To most Americans, the Kennedy family needs no introduction. They are known for many things ncluding, being in politics, having a large family, wealth, and various scandals, but they are probably most known for the horrific assassinations of President John F. Kennedy (1963) and his younger brother and presidential candidate, Senator Robert F. Kennedy (1968). The Kennedy brothers were both gunned down in broad daylight for all the country (and world) to see. I was very young when both events occurred, but I do remember them (like those old enough to remember 9/11). I'm not mentioning these events to delve into politics or the who, what, when, and why of these awful tragedies. What I am getting at here is the heartache, grief, and devastating pain mother Rose Kennedy (and family) experienced twice over. Yet, in her autobiography, *Times to Remember*,[1] we read her words explaining though the pain never goes away, she decided that she would not allow these events to control or define her life because that would take away her example of strength in the toughest of times. She said she decided not to be overcome by circumstances because she wanted to be an example of strength for others facing difficult times in their life.

Viktor Frankl is another example. In his book, *Man's Search for Meaning*,[2] Viktor Frankl suffered years of torture and the worst of inhumane treatment as a prisoner in the Nazi concentration camps. His story is one of daily dread, depression, desolation, soul-destruction, and death all around him. Yet, Dr. Frankl witnessed that even in the worst environmental conditions, man still has a choice of action and attitude. He said that although everything can be taken from a man there is one thing that cannot be taken and that is choosing one's own attitude and one's own way under *any* circumstance.

This is an extreme example to be sure, but nevertheless still relevant to our ability and power we have as human beings *to choose* one's attitude in the worst of circumstances.

I hope you find this human capacity we have *to choose* as enlightening and empowering as I do. It liberates me from the victim mentality. It proves that I can do something about my circumstances. Unlike animals, I can choose my thoughts and response to what happens to me rather than being controlled by my feelings and reacting instinctively like animals. If I'm not happy with how my life is today, I don't have to accept it. The truth is, where I've been in my past, and where I'm at in my life today, may not necessarily be *my fate* that was always meant to be, especially if I'm barely hanging on and suffering through my daily existence.

In POM, we teach all parents—biological, stepparents and otherwise—that we are meant to thrive in life, not just survive in life and when it comes to raising my children, stepchildren, and building my blended family life, I am not a victim of my past life. I can choose to overcome and create a better life for my blended family.

I want to end this section with a few principles to remember about the power of choice as we learn how to know ourselves and grow in emotional maturity:

- My state of mind or being is not so much due to what happens to me as much as what I choose to do about what happens to me.
- I can choose how I feel about what happens to me.
- I can choose how to think about what happens to me.
- I am not my feelings. I have feelings but my feelings don't define me.
- I am not my mood. I have moods by my moods don't define me.
- Temperament is not destiny. My genetic and/or ethnic make-up does not determine who I become.
- I can choose to respond positively and not react negatively under stressful situations.

Blended families and stepparenting arise from diverse circumstances, each presenting its own unique challenges and pressures. While every family's journey is different, one powerful principle remains constant: the ability to choose your attitude and shape a positive path forward. By embracing this mindset, you can navigate the complexities of blending families without allowing challenges to create division, ensuring that your approach fosters unity rather than conflict.

D. The Power of Forgiveness and Living in Our Potential

When I teach about forgiveness, I always tell people that if they choose not to forgive, then they need to understand and accept the fact that they're choosing to live their lives in an *emotional wheelchair*. I know that sounds harsh, but this is serious stuff we're talking about here.

We've all seen someone who is living life in a wheelchair either because they were born that way or because some tragic accident happened that caused them to be crippled and therefore never able to live up to their *physical* potential. However, being born crippled or having an accident is not a choice. But when we choose not to forgive, we are choosing that emotional wheelchair, and we just need to accept the fact that we will never live in our full human potential that way. It's impossible.

Our emotional life is powerful and must be allowed to express itself and connect with other humans on a purely relational level. Just as it's impossible for a crippled person to ever live in their physical potential, it's impossible for an unforgiving person to live in their emotional potential, and this cripples many, if not all, of their relationships. So, again, I know that's a hard pill to swallow, but if it wasn't so important for your personal growth and development and relationship with yourself and your kids, I wouldn't give it to you.

Having said all that, I realize the decision to forgive does not come as easy for some as for others. Fair enough. In cases like this, I make these suggestions:

1. If you are in a place where you are simply not ready or able to forgive, then I suggest you at least begin to consider the act of forgiveness for your own emotional growth and health.
2. The next step is to simply seek for the desire—the willingness—to let go of the anger and bitterness. As you continue sincerely asking for and seeking the grace and strength to forgive and let go, it will come, and you will be set free.
3. Another reason people won't forgive is because they confuse forgiveness with trust. But they are two different things. Remember, forgiveness is free, but trust must always be earned. If you choose to forgive someone who has violated your trust, you will be free from resentment towards him or her, but they are still in your debt to earn your trust by proving their character over a reasonable amount of time. Don't forget that forgiving someone doesn't mean you have to trust them, too.
4. Another reason people are reluctant to forgive is they think that by forgiving their perpetrator they are *letting them get away with it* or endorsing their behavior. But the hard truth is, by holding on to your resentment, bitterness, and unforgiveness, you are not only allowing them to get away with it, but also choosing to let him, her, or them control your life and relationships. Thus, to encourage you to consider forgiving and letting it go, I ask you: Who is the one

hurting and suffering by hanging on to the past you can't change?

Once we understand that hanging onto unforgiveness is controlling and hindering our personal potential, we come to understand that the choice to forgive is for our own good. To heal from past wounds and hurts, it helps us to make that liberating choice to forgive.

I can't think of a better example of the power of forgiveness than the life story of South Africa's best-known and loved heroic leader, Nelson Mandela. If you're still having trouble with the issue of forgiving, I believe learning more about his story (and other stories like his) can help inspire you to look at things a bit differently. To put this in perspective, let me tell you a little more about his background.

As a young man he led his community in their struggle for racial equality. He was a founding member of the African National Congress and held many other positions in other organizations formed to win their battle against prejudice and discrimination. The fact is his only crime was his opposition to the injustices of governmental racism, hatred, discrimination, and prejudice towards his people.

In the beginning of his struggle, he organized peaceful resistance in the form of civil disobedience. Later, when the peaceful resistance strategy was not working, he decided that the only choice left to him was armed resistance for which he was eventually arrested and given a life sentence. In 1963, he was put into a prison cell to quiet his voice and end his threat to the government. However, his imprisonment only served to strengthen his voice of influence, as he became the most respected leader in South Africa while in prison.

Years of civil pressure on the government to release him became overwhelming, and he was finally released from prison in 1990. Four years later, in May of 1994, he became the first democratically elected black president of South Africa.

After learning about all the injustices this man went through, no one would fault him for being full of hatred and wanting revenge on his persecutors. Once he came into power as the president of the country, we could expect him to hunt down his persecutors and take his revenge. But Nelson Mandela was not your normal leader. After being elected president, he did not attack or go after his political oppressors seeking revenge. Instead, he preached a message of peace, forgiveness, and reconciliation.

In 2009, Mandela's life story was made into a movie, *Invictus*. If you haven't seen it, I highly recommend that you do. His actions of peace ended the decade's old racist policy of the South African government known as "Apartheid"—a government based on laws of racial oppression and segregation. For his long life's struggle and political policies of peace and unity among all South Africans, he was awarded the Nobel Peace Prize in 1993, an award given each year to the person regarded as further influencing peaceful negotiations and relationships on a global level.

In speaking about how he felt about his enemies who had imprisoned him for all those years, he talked about how holding on to revenge was the same as drinking poison in hopes that it would kill your enemy. I just love that saying of his. It's such a liberating, life-changing, powerful truth.

Mandela experienced and understood what unforgiveness does to a person. Eventually, he discovered the freedom even a man in prison can receive from the power of forgiveness. He's an example for all who have suffered injustice and how we can overcome anger and revenge towards those who have hurt and violated us and find the grace in our hearts to forgive and live in our full potential.

Along the path of our lives, we are going to suffer being hurt by someone in one way or another. Especially in our stepparent and blended family situation, there are plenty of opportunities to be hurt. How we choose to deal with those hurts, however, is the key to whether we are a victim of our hurts or a victor over them.

Ultimately, choosing to forgive is an act of our will. It is not a feeling necessarily. It is knowing that if I want to be free and not live as a victim to my past, I must choose to let it go, forgive, and move forward to living in my full potential.

Principles for a Lifestyle of Forgiving:

- **Like any other skill, forgiveness must be desired.** The desire comes from my understanding that I'm hanging on to something that is causing unhappiness in my life.
- **Forgiving must be learned.** It is unnatural to forgive others that violate our trust or cause us physical or emotional pain. But once we see the freedom

forgiving brings us, it helps us to make the decision to forgive even when our negative thoughts are telling us not to.

- **Forgiving must be demonstrated.** Showing forgiveness is one of the most powerful things a parent can demonstrate to their children. The example of a parent forgiving their spouse, in-laws, siblings, and their children goes a long way in building a happy, healthy home culture.

- **Forgiving must be nurtured.** As I said above, to forgive someone who has hurt me in some way is counter-intuitive to our human nature. It is much easier to not forgive and justify our resentment. Therefore, unless we are continually nurturing this attitude, it will continue to be a struggle.

- **Forgiving must be continuously practiced.** We live in an imperfect world, and therefore we will have plenty of opportunities to practice and get better and better at letting go of the things other people do or say that cause us emotional suffering.

- **The power in the principle of forgiveness is experienced in three ways:**
    1. Being forgiven by someone you have offended.
    2. Forgiving others who have offended you.
    3. Forgiving self for past regrets and wrongdoing and/or hurtful acts you committed.

Personally, it's the third point that has caused me my biggest challenge. I have caused deep hurt before in others that I care for and love and this can weigh heavy on one's conscience. It requires real sincerity and consistent faith to believe and accept forgiveness from others and from yourself. This is another reason why the work we do with controlling our thoughts and negative self-talk is so important. If we don't exercise our faith and accept that we are truly forgiven, our mind can condemn, ridicule, and cause us to become depressed with a very low self-image. This feeling of shame and/or guilt ends up affecting our relationships with our children, family, friends, and our co-workers.

This principle of forgiving is so crucial and yet so overlooked as a major reason why families, blended families, parent-child relationships, and other human relationships become so problematic, toxic, and dysfunctional. Furthermore, we all know that the behavior we model to our children has a deep impression upon their character and behavior, especially in how they treat others. Demonstrating a character that is unwilling to choose to forgive can become generational. It's an attitude potentially passed down to your children as a justified way of treating others who make mistakes, err in one way or another, or fail to meet our expectations. But we can break that cycle by choosing to forgive.

Finally, I want to express two important points to remember about forgiveness:

- The choice to forgive someone who has violated you does not require an apology. In my case, my father was long gone and yet I decided to forgive him without an apology from him or any other kind of acknowledgement from him for his wrongdoing towards me, my mom, and my siblings.

- Forgiving ourselves does not require that we receive forgiveness from those we have hurt. We cannot rely on others for our healthy relationship with ourselves. Guilt, shame, and blame are major hurdles we struggle with to overcome because we think we need approval or affirmation from those we have offended. Not so. Ideally, that would be nice. But the reality is that offended people are not always as gracious as we would hope them to be, and we cannot allow ourselves to be held emotionally hostage by their unforgiving spirit.

Everyone *sins*. No one is perfect and therefore no one has the right to hold another in his or her debt for life as if they themselves have never committed the same or similar offenses to others. If you seek, but don't receive, forgiveness from someone you have hurt, do not allow that to be the defining factor for your own acquittal. Learn from your mistakes, seek the inner faith and strength to forgive yourself, and keep growing and moving forward.

I end this chapter with a powerful example of how the POM curriculum helps get people to this choice to forgive and, in many cases, cause reconciliation.

I was teaching POM in the women's section of the Lerdo jail in Bakersfield. I had ended the session and challenged the class to write a letter, if needed, as a way to express their feelings fully and put into use what they had learned about forgiving and letting go of the past so they could grasp onto a better future. When I returned the following day to teach, one of the women handed me a letter she had written as I had suggested. She wanted me to read it, so I did. When I finished reading it, I tried to hand it back to her, but she refused and said, "No. I don't need it now. I'm free. I just wanted you to know how much this has helped me."

At that I asked her if I could keep the letter to use an as an example for others to which she agreed. Here is what she wrote to her biological mother:

> *I want you to know that I have never claimed you as my mother. The way I see it is you have never done anything to earn that title. Allow me to explain. When you remarried a single man with three kids, making us all one big "Brady Bunch," I was only two years old, the youngest of us all. You never stuck up for me to either [the name of her stepfather] or his three spoiled, bratty children. They were always right. I was always wrong, so I grew up always being called a liar and never having a voice. Your desire to win their acceptance as wife and new mother, was at the expense of never having a relationship with me. They were very cruel to me, and you were all I had to protect me but you didn't. You are a coward. Even to this day you are still bowing down to him.*
>
> *Luckily, my real father's girlfriend stepped up to*

the plate and became a mother to me and I've been blessed to grow into the kind and loving woman I am today. That's why I'm writing you this letter. To release the anger I have been holding against you in my heart so I may grow more in maturity. I do have a love for you, because to be honest with myself I'm not perfect and have made many mistakes that I am now paying for as I am sure you are also. So, I forgive you for it all and will keep forgiving you daily as long as it takes.

Sincerely, [Her name]

Now you might be thinking, *But Richard. If she gave the original letter to you that means her mother never received the letter from her.* That's correct, which makes the point I made earlier about the power of forgiveness in that to experience this freedom you neither need an apology nor do you need the other person to be in your life. The power of forgiveness isn't dependent on others. It is an individual decision that liberates you whether the perpetrator is aware, alive, or not.

Some things are harder to forgive than others. But to live freely, I must forgive. Some people are harder to forgive than others. But to live in my full potential as a human being, I must forgive. I urge you today to choose to live in your full potential!

CHAPTER TEN
Earning Respect as a Stepparent- Balancing Authority and Influence

When I consider the issue of why kids go astray, I believe one of the most overlooked reasons for why this happens is the lack of, or misuse of, parental authority. Once again, usually when kids act out or make negative lifestyle choices, we tend to put our focus and efforts on changing their behavior, rather than looking in the mirror and asking if perhaps we are part of the problem. Of course, this requires the consistent practice and application of the emotional maturity exercises I covered earlier. Many parents have either lost their child's respect for their authority, or they don't consistently and properly exercise it in the first place.

In her book, *Adult Children of Emotionally Immature Parents*, Lindsay C. Gibson discusses how parents who are emotionally immature don't do well under stressful situations.[1] One can imagine how much more stressful stepparenting can be when trying to blend families, especially when dealing with disobedient, rebellious children who challenge their authority for any number of reasons.

Furthermore, parental authority has been undermined, diminished, and increasingly attacked as inappropriate in certain social settings. For example, public schools instituting policies that keep parents ignorant of important subject matters being taught, or life changing decisions their kids are making with the guidance of school counselors like gender identification issues, safe-sex practices, and/or abortions without parental consent.

This undermining of parental authority has been a societal pressure on parents that just seems to keep growing with intensity. The parental voice of authority is being drowned out by schools, social agencies, and government. Many parents are scared to exercise their authority with their children as they fear they might come under the scrutiny and judgment of these entities. They do not feel supported in exercising their rights to have a say in their child's education, discipline, social media exposure, and time engaging with peers over social media platforms.

In their book, *Hold On to Your Kids, Why Parents Need to Matter More Than Peers*, Gordon Nuefeld, Ph.D., and Gabor Mate, M.D., discuss the competition parents face that is pulling their kids away from them and how today's parents do not have the support from *the village* they once did[2], which makes their relationship with their children/stepchildren all the more important.

One very clear message I teach in POM is that parents are not only the number one asset in the community, but they are also the final authority in the lives of their children. That is their rightful position in their home. It is their rightful position with their children in public, whether that be at the doctor's office, dentist's office, school principal's office, church office, or coach's office. This is a position of authority they should hold onto and never abdicate to other authorities in the community. Yet, sadly, many parents do exactly that due to the pressures mentioned above.

In POM we have a slogan that says, "It does NOT take a village to raise a child. It just takes good parents." When I first share this slogan people look at me funny because most know the popular saying, "It takes a village to raise a child." But does it really? Then I ask, "Well, if that's true how, many of you are willing to turn your child over to the village? The community?"

Nobody ever raises their hand. I then go on to explain that this popular phrase, "It takes a village to raise a child" is a good thought and well meaning. But it was meant for a different time and a different culture. The truth is, unfortunately, we are not even sure who we can trust anymore, whether it's the White House, the schoolhouse, the churchhouse, or even the law enforcement house.

Without a doubt, we welcome the community's help and support. However, the responsibility of raising my children rests solely on me—not the teachers, counselors, coaches, pastors, or priests. That is the message we want to instill in parents: *You are the parent. You hold the responsibility, and You are enough!*

And, from a stepparent perspective, if you exercise your authority wisely, you can create a lasting impact. And, consider this, while it may not take a village to raise a child, one child can raise up an entire village. Who knows? You may be raising the very child who will transform a whole community—just as we have seen with leaders like Dr. Martin Luther King Jr., Cesar Chavez, and many others.

On the other side of this coin, it must be said that obviously parents can lose their position of authority with their children if they, or their children, break the rules, social mores, and/or laws that we are all subject to in a healthy society, which is all the more reason why the proper use of parental authority is so vital in raising obedient, happy, healthy, and productive children.

The Proper Use of Authority

While parental authority is vital to raising happy and respectful children, it is the proper and improper use of authority that needs to be addressed and understood by parents.

Many parents mistake *power* for authority, but they are two different things. Power implies coercion, and the ability to force someone against their will to do what you want them to do. In the context of small toddlers, who tend to do the wrong thing, say the wrong thing, and be in the wrong place at the wrong time, endangering their well-being, employing your parental power for their own good is understood. But as children grow in their understanding, it becomes necessary for parents to influence their children with their moral authority, not power. Authority is about influencing others to willingly follow or obey your instructions. This is what we want our children to respond to. Not our parental power, but rather our parental authority.

Three Basic Styles to Parenting

Over the years, experts have identified various parenting styles, each with its unique approach to raising children. Let's explore these three styles first explained by Diana Baumrind, a prominent clinical and developmental psychologist, after she conducted extensive research in the 1960s that led to the identification of three primary parenting styles.[3]

- **Authoritarian**—This is a controlling style with no room for discussion. The authoritarian parent does not allow or want input from children. The rules and expectations are what they are, and fear is the main tactic to get compliance. The child is not encouraged to express their feelings or their point of view. The parents' decisions and actions are always right, especially when it comes to discipline.
- **Permissive**—A permissive parent is almost the exact opposite of the authoritarian. Much warmth and affection are given to children. However, the permissive parent refrains from offering guidance or direction. Children are left free to express their emotions, attitudes, and tantrums with no consequences. The parent does not see themselves in a position of authority or as someone responsible for

shaping character. They accept the child as is and allow children to regulate their own attitudes. They avoid confrontation.

- **Authoritative**—This style of parenting is a balance between the authoritarian and the permissive parent. They set high standards but also provide a lot of warmth, encouragement, and empathy when appropriate. As children mature, they explain and discuss the reason for their decisions and actions and include their children in house rules and disciplinary action as appropriate. They confront children, hold them accountable to family values and obedience to authority figures, and take an active role in shaping character.

Authoritative style of parenting is what we advocate in POM as the proper use of authority that earns respect and obedience.

Authoritative parenting requires emotional maturity on the part of the parent not the child. With an authoritarian style, parents are borrowing from their power. As I stated earlier, using this technique with older children, parents may get their way, but they will weaken their relationship and miss the opportunity to earn respect and obedience to their authority.

Benefits of Authoritative Parenting

Authoritative parenting establishes:

- **The foundation of moral character**–In the early years of childhood, the parents' voice can be likened to the voice of a child's conscience. You are providing guidance, direction, and a sense of right and wrong. Good decisions and bad decisions. Acceptable social conduct vs. unacceptable social conduct.

○ **A sense of security**–When the unfamiliar, unexpected, chaotic, and/or tragic happen, it is our natural instinct to look for assurance of survival and security. Any American who experienced 9/11 as a youth, teen, or adult remembers the state of the country when that tragic and dramatic terror attack took place. The country was shaken to its core. Normal major events like NFL games were cancelled and houses of worship had record attendance (though it was short-lived). But what Americans were really looking for was the security of those in authority, such as the government and the military, to stand up and reassure us that we would get through this catastrophe and be okay. As parents who have been exercising authority, nurturing, and guidance, our children will naturally look to us in times of disturbance for security.

○ **Respect for the honor of others**–This is something that children must be taught. Whenever we had company over to our home, it was normal for our small children to pay no attention or give no recognition to our guests. This was an ongoing lesson I had to teach my children especially when their grandparents would visit. I would have to call them in from outside or from out of their rooms and away from their video games just to come and acknowledge their grandparents, say "HI" and give a hug and a kiss. Basically, show respect and honor to our house guests. As my children got older, this was their automatic response, and I no longer had to encourage them. But I can tell you that this is not the norm in a lot of homes with a lot of children. Why? Because their children have no respect for their parents' authority as they have been too permissive on a regular basis and then when it comes time for them to try and get their children to comply, the children ignore them.

○ **Concern for the welfare of others**–Another thing that children must be taught. Years ago, when one of my stepsons was about ten or eleven years old, I told him I wanted him to go across the street and tell our neighbor that from now on he was going to pull her big trash can down to the curb on trash day for her. He looked at me like I was crazy and said, "What?" Our neighbor across the street was an elderly woman and her husband had recently passed away. One day I saw her struggling to pull her garbage can down her driveway and onto the street as we all do on trash day. So, I thought this was a good opportunity to teach my stepson about being a good neighbor. Did he want to do it? No. But did he do it? Yes. Was it because I was being a mean, authoritarian stepparent? No. I was teaching him about being a good neighbor and having concern for the welfare of others. To do that

I exercised my authority and explained to him why I was telling him to do a kindness for our neighbor.

Respect for Parental Authority

Before I share some principles on how to earn respect for your authority, I want to take the time here to share a couple of caveats:

> In order for you to earn respect for your authority, it will require you to commit to practicing the personal growth principles I shared in chapter one. I cannot emphasize this enough. This is the key to implementing the foundational principles I am sharing here. Knowing and understanding what to do is one thing, but the discipline of doing the internal work of personal growth in emotional maturity is quite another.

None of us are perfect and no parent/stepparent gets it right all the time. That is an unrealistic expectation for parents raising another human being. Those of us who have experienced parenthood know that no two children are alike, even with the same biological parents, let alone stepchildren. Temperaments, personalities, character, disposition, etc. are one way with one child and another way with another child. Although it is sometimes true that two children can be very alike in some ways, I would say that is the exception and not the rule. Therefore, I want to be clear on this point because too many parents/stepparents beat themselves up, become disappointed and/or depressed when things don't go well, and feel they are losing the battle of healthy child-rearing with one or more of their children.

The principles I share in POM are sound, but they are not a 100 percent guarantee that all will go well 100 percent of the time. But I do believe, and have experienced personally with other POM graduates, that if you put in the time to practice the personal growth principles shared in POM (and/or all the other variety of emotional growth resources available in books, classes, and online courses out there), you are giving yourself a very optimistic expectation for raising happy, healthy, productive children/stepchildren. You are in the best position to influence and shape the character of your children, and your growth in emotional maturity is the key.

Secondly, regarding respect for and obedience to your authority, I want to remind you that you have a head start with your babies and small children. I call it the "Home Field Advantage" (I will cover this in more detail in the next section). But for now, I want to encourage you that, in my opinion, children inherently desire to love, respect, and obey their parents. Of course, this is more challenging for stepchildren, and is not *inherent*, but it is something that we can win over time if we are consistent in practicing the principles I am sharing about personal growth in emotional maturity. Why wouldn't these desires grow with our stepchildren if they are receiving attention, affection, and love? As the natural process of daily life unfolds, parents and children form a strong emotional attachment that meets the need that all human beings have, which is to belong. To be a valued member of the family. As children grow, they instinctively know they need support, guidance, rules, discipline, and care. Having said that, the mistake we can make sometimes is taking the innate desire for granted, not realizing that this desire still needs to be cultivated, nurtured, and brought to fruition. How that is done is what I want to share with you next.

Principles for Earning Respect for Parental Authority
It is important to realize that although our children will misbehave, they will also want to reconcile and know they are secure in our unconditional love. However, reconciling is not something most young children will know how to do unless we model and communicate this with them. One adage I teach parents is: *When our children do the wrong thing, we must do the right thing.* Of course, the *right thing* can mean many different things depending on the situation. But, in general, what I'm expressing here and reminding parents of is that the misbehavior of our children are opportunities for growth and the exercising of our emotional growth to respond in appropriate ways rather than emotionally reacting in ways that can make the situation worse. Remember: We can fight fire with water, and fight fire with fire, but we never want to fight fire with the emotion of *gasoline*.

Principle number One: Decide that a good relationship is more important than being right.

After a confrontation, parents have an opportunity to set the example of humility. To exercise humility will usually take some time to cool down and re-think how we have handled the situation. The truth is that oftentimes how we handled the confrontation was not good. We are at fault for the words we used and how we reacted to a difficult situation. Or, even after re-thinking it all, we may still conclude that we were in *the right*. Here is where we need to be aware of choosing to be stubborn because being right does not always build relationships and that is the more important point.

The more important issue is restoring a healthy understanding with our child. We can achieve this through calmer communication as an attempt to reconcile our differences regardless of who is right or wrong.

Some parents might not buy into this and reject this with an attitude of, *too bad, they will just have to get over it*. But oftentimes our children don't, and this stubborn attitude can cause our child to harbor resentment and begin to disrespect us, not because they think they are always right, but because we do.

Usually, kids know when they are in the wrong. However, what they are reacting to is our disrespect for their views and a devaluation of their child development process. Thus, for the relationships sake I suggest that you:

- Calm down and think beyond who is right or wrong, and consider if there was a better way to handle the situation.
- Go back and listen again to their side of things and make sure they feel heard and understood. Remember: understanding their point of view does not mean we have to agree.

These actions build relationships and respect, and helps you maintain your role as the primary authority figure in their life. Most kids will respond to this type of exercising of authority and respect us for our humility, fairness, and willingness to hear them out. The clear message this sends is how much we value them as individuals and how much we want a healthy and meaningful relationship with them that goes beyond having to be right.

Principle number Two: Admit when you are wrong and apologize.

After practicing the *art of listening*, we may discover that we were, in fact, wrong in our thoughts, words, and deeds—plain and simple and no excuses. Again, this is why our emotional maturity is so important because oftentimes our mistakes as parents are a result of jumping to wrong conclusions.

After we listen to our kids under more emotional control, we know they are right and only our pride will keep us from admitting to ourselves, and to them, that we were in the wrong.

Another way we can come to realize that we were wrong is when our conscience begins to bother us because of the way we handled a situation with our child.

For example, there were times when I would get into it with one of my children or stepchildren. Arguing, yelling, saying things out of anger, slamming doors, etc. (Maybe you know what I'm talking about?). Once the argument ended, I would go sit down and either begin to read, or watch TV, or just find something else to do. But in the quietness of those moments, that still small voice would begin to speak to me, i.e., my conscience began to bother me saying, *you didn't handle that well. You didn't listen to your daughter. You lost your temper again and you need to go back, apologize, and make this right.*

Now, at that point, I had a decision to make. Either I was going to listen and obey my conscience—or I wasn't. And the worst part about it was even if I shrugged it off and just continued to do what I was doing that still small voice wouldn't go away . . . not right away.

This is a prime example of what I'm referring to about emotional maturity and why my continuing on the path of personal growth is so important. Emotionally immature people don't listen to their conscience. That's a dangerous place to be because if you choose to continue to ignore your conscience, you end up dulling its voice, deceiving yourself, and now you are left to your own immature mind, which is not a heatlhy place to be as a parent/stepparent if you care about living in your full potential and building a healthy family culture.

Emotionally mature people respond to their conscience and do what it takes to make things right. Once we know that we were in the wrong, it's time for the humility to look our child in the eye, admit to them we were wrong, apologize, and ask for forgiveness. When children witness authority figures admit to their mistakes and apologize for them, it goes a long way in establishing respect for you and, ultimately, your authority.

Principle number Three: Be flexible, fair, and firm.

Know the difference between mistakes or accidents and defiance or willful disobedience.

As parents, sometimes we can be guilty of *choking on the ant but swallowing the camel*. In other words, we make the little things big things and the big things little. For example, as our children get older, they come under more peer pressure to fit in, be cool, and join the *in crowd, as we used to call it back in the day*. Now, your daughter has graduated from elementary school and is in middle school. One day she comes out of her room to go to school, and you hardly recognize her. Her hair is different. Her clothes are different, and she is wearing facial makeup. In other words, she's growing up and is trying to fit in with her friends and other girls her age at school. But that's not how you see it. You're surprised. You react in anger. You start yelling and saying hurtful things about how she looks, and demand that she goes back to her room, change her clothes, and take off the makeup. Embarrassed and humiliated, she runs back to her room in tears.

The next day you're watching television, and you overhear your wife tell your daughter to wash the dishes. Your daughter gets upset and says she doesn't want to. Now mom gets upset and starts arguing with her. Eventually, in the heat of the moment, your daughter refuses to comply and is talking back disrespectfully and tells her mom to *shut up* and she storms out of the kitchen. And you . . . do nothing and say nothing. Now which of these two incidents is *the ant* and which is *the camel*?

Is the reality of my daughter growing up and trying to find her way amongst her peers the bigger issue? Or is it the tone of voice she uses towards her mother and talking back to her in such a disrespectful manner? In the first scenario, you saw this as a major issue to the point of reacting in a way of putting your daughter down and humiliating her to tears. In the second scenario, you saw this as no big deal and just sat there continuing to watch TV as your wife, her mother, was disrespected by her daughter . . . no big deal, right? I don't think so.

Don't get me wrong. I understand that our children might go too far at times when they are under peer pressure to fit in. And at that point we can intervene and provide some parental guidance. A young girl changing her hair style, clothes, and putting on makeup is a normal stage of growth. And, not wanting to do house chores and talking back to a parent is a normal (for some, not all teens) stage of growth as well. Now this may not be the best example, but I think you get my point.

I suppose one could say that a change in hairstyle, clothes, and makeup doesn't fall under the category of a mistake or accident, but certainly refusing to obey a parent asking a child to do their chores and then talking back in a disrespectful manner is willful defiance that in my view cannot go unchecked by a parent and deserves a firm response and potential consequences. The former issue, in my opinion, is an opportunity for flexibility and a fair discussion to show our teen that we understand, we've been there, and we just want to be sure they don't take it too far, which most teens will understand when that type of message is delivered in a calm manner.

Kids are very tuned in to unfairness or injustice and have a keen sense of what is a mountain and what is a molehill. To avoid unfairness or injustice when dealing with our kids, I believe, is a matter of maintaining a flexible and fair posture. This takes perception, insight, knowledge, and experience but it also requires the flexibility to listen to your kids to learn how to discern different situations. The key here is that kids know that you have the final word, yet you are allowing them to judge themselves and this is where you can gain respect, earn loyalty, and create emotional bonds that pay big dividends later down the road when it counts. Through being flexible, fair, and firm, we open the opportunities to develop character, increase the level of the relationship, and seize moments for a lesson in leadership and the proper use of authority. Thus, the battle for establishing respect for parental authority is a must and must be handled correctly, consistently, fairly, and firmly.

CHAPTER ELEVEN

The Home Field Advantage
Building Strong Attachments That Counter External Influences

I developed this strategy out of a burden to give parents an answer when they would ask me, *Mr. Ramos, how can I prevent my younger children from following in the footsteps of their older brother/sister that is already* . . . then they would describe whatever negative lifestyle one or more of their older children were involved in: drugs, gangs, dropping out of school, rebellious and/or violent behavior at home or at school, etc. These parents feared their younger children would also get involved and wanted to prevent this. But at first, I didn't have an answer.

As I mentioned earlier, as the at-risk counselor at the school I was a young parent myself. I hadn't experienced any of my children going astray, so I couldn't really give any credible counsel, and that bothered me . . . a lot.

I would go home and think about it. One of those things that *keeps you up at night*. I didn't want to give some unrealistic, corny advice, yet I knew there had to be something I could come up with that was realistic based on the same principles I was using with my own kids.

I did some research and discovered that most kids who go astray do so between the ages of twelve to fifteen years old. That caused me to have one of those ah-ha moments. I thought, if that in fact was true, that the ages for kids most at risk for making bad choices began at the age of twelve, that meant parents should have an advantage for twelve years before their *competition steps on their field*, so to speak.

Having been an athlete, I tend to think in sports metaphors. And the more I thought about it, I saw the temptations and peer pressures for this time frame as the *competition* and the twelve years before the competition became a threat, as an advantage parents should have in the battle of peer pressure—*if* they knew what to do during this crucial time frame. Thus, I call it the Home Field Advantage since most of the time small children, from infancy to twelve years old, are under the care and influence of their parents at home.

If you are not a sports fan, having the home field advantage is important in giving an edge to winning a game, especially big games like a playoff or championship game. Being able to play on your home field, with most of the fans in the stadium on your side and being familiar with the nuances of the field (or court) you practice on every day, can give you an edge in the competition of a game, not to mention the fact that the referees are on your side too (That's kind of a joke . . . but then again, referees are human. I'll just leave it there).

I then thought through a time frame of twelve years and not only what parents must do, but also how to do what they must do to maximize this twelve-year window of opportunity. I broke up the twelve years into three different time frames:

- Infant–two years old
- Two years old–five years old
- Five years old–twelve years old

The question I answered for the parent was what should be happening in the life of a child during each of these key time frames? The following is what we teach parents in the POM classes.

Parents are Gardeners of the Soul. Time Frame: Infant–two years old.

I like to use the term "gardener" because it speaks to the skill of nurturing and cultivating that is vital for a child's well-being, especially during this specific time frame.

Infants, toddlers, and preschool children have no concept of negative lifestyles—therefore, there is no competition . . . yet, but parents must seize this time frame to cultivate, nurture, and ground the roots of the soul during these most impressionable years.

Psychologist Ann Miller says in her book, *The Drama of the Gifted Child*, it is absolutely vital that the mother is not separated from her newborn.[1] This is a period of time when the mother's hormones are flourishing, and her motherly instincts are released immediately after birth and continue in the following days. Thus, if a newborn is separated from his/her mother at the time of birth, a great opportunity is missed for both mother and child to bond and form the psychological and emotional attachment and feeling of oneness that ideally has been growing from the time of conception. The infant is given the sense of safety he needs to trust his mother.

Furthermore, according to First 5 California, an organization with a mission to support and optimize early childhood development, they advocate for parents to: *Talk. Read. Sing*[2] from day one to enhance the child's brain connections that determine how they will learn, think, and grow. Thus, during this time frame parents should be *gardening the soul* by nurturing:

- The tenderness of emotions
- The reasoning of the mind
- The loyalty of their free will
- Emotional security
- Emotional self-worth
- Emotional stability

Parent tool for Nurturing: All forms of affection including cuddling, holding, hugging, kissing, talking, reading, and singing.

This tool of affection may seem too simplistic. But the truth is many parents do not know how to be affectionate. That was my experience when I first became a parent. I didn't know how to be affectionate mostly because my mother was not affectionate, and, as it turns out, neither were her parents affectionate with her. My mother once told me that she felt bad about this because she realized that she was not a very affectionate mother. She told me a story about my grandfather who never told her he loved her or showed her any kind of affection.

One day, as she recalled, she was leaving home for school in the morning. As she walked down her front porch and began walking down the street, she noticed her father walking toward her. As they got closer, she looked at him to greet him, but he just ignored her and kept on walking past her. She called out, "Papa. It's me, your daughter. Aren't you going to say 'Hi'?"

But he just continued walking and ignoring her.

Unfortunately, this is not an uncommon experience for far too many children. And then we become parents and lack this vital ability to give our children what they need because we don't have it. That's the bad news. However, the good news is that being affectionate can be learned. But even if a parent struggles to be affectionate, a child can receive it from others in their life such as extended family members and/or other caring adults in their life.

I know this is true because I experienced it. I watched how my wife and Sicilian in-laws smothered my children with so much love and affection that it used to make me uncomfortable. I had never seen such affection . . . a constant and continuous attention, touching, hugging, holding, and kissing practically the whole time they were with my children, especially when they were in this infant to two-year old time frame. They made up for whatever affection my children were lacking from me. But I did eventually learn to be an affectionate father and remain so today, and so can you! Never underestimate the powerful effect of the need for physical touch, hugs, and kisses by your children.

Parents are Trainers of Obedience.
Time frame: Two to five years old.

One of the things I enjoy doing is planting flowers and different types of vines and watching them grow to their full maturity. I like the vines that grow and crawl on fences, walls, guard rails, and wherever else I train and want them to grow.

The tricky part about potting and/or planting flowers and plants is getting them securely rooted in the right soil and sunlight. Transplanting from a pot into the ground, or a bigger pot, is a delicate process and doesn't go well if you don't treat them with sensitivity. When I first started this hobby, I wasted a lot of money buying the wrong plants and discovering that they would not grow because of the temperature during the different parts of the year where I was living. But once I learned which plants did well in certain climates and learned the proper process of planting and transplanting, I knew the roots were happy and healthy because my plants flowered beautifully to full maturity.

All of this takes consistent attention, care, shaping, and pruning. And I believe the same principles apply for the healthy growth of children. The roots of their soul are vital to their full development and that is where our full attention, care, and shaping of character needs to be. It's not about controlling or domineering every aspect of your child's individuality. But just as plants will not do well without proper care of their roots, neither will children without the proper care of their character. Yet, as all parents know, this next time frame can prove to be very challenging, and I find, oftentimes, too many parents give up and give in and neglect this important role, which is a big mistake.

At two-years-old, children are now very aware of what's happening and usually begin to challenge a parent's authority. They want what they want, when they want it, how they want it, and where they want it . . . now! The self and selfishness are alive and well and on full display towards both parents, siblings, and other playmates. So, now what?

Parents in this time frame must maintain the gardener role but add to it the role of what I call a "Trainer." Those of you who exercise regularly or belong to a physical workout program understand what I mean by having a Trainer. That person who knows you and knows what you are trying to achieve mentally, physically, and spiritually, and is there to encourage, push, and keep you on a disciplined regiment to achieve your goals.

Obviously, a two-year-old child doesn't have these types of goals, but the same principle of needing a Trainer applies to help them develop a healthy character and sense of self, rather than allowing them to grow like a wild, unnurtured, and uncultivated plant that never grew to its potential because of unhealthy roots.

Educating the Conscience

The shaping of character is essentially a process of training the conscience. Everybody is born with a conscience. This is a natural part of our humanity in knowing the difference between right and wrong. However, having a strong obedience to, or weak response to, our conscience is an individual matter, not the same for everyone, and parents are in the best position to provide this education. Thus, as parents, when we see or hear our child unknowingly putting themselves in danger, we quickly stop them to educate them that touching a hot stove or playing too close to the street is harmful to them. When we hear them being impolite and/or saying bad words, we correct them to let them know the correct and incorrect use of words. If our children disrespect our neighbors, we correct them. If they act out in school, we take responsibility and enact potential consequences to teach them proper social mores. In other words, the motivation of our parental voice of correction as their initial trainer, educator, and voice of conscience is for the betterment of themselves in the following areas:

- Respect for self
- Respect for others
- Respect for authority
- Respect for boundaries

We know the unsettling inside our hearts when our conscience is bothering us for doing the wrong thing. We also know the calming peace and serenity gained when we have obeyed our conscience and done the right thing. Doing the right thing, and doing things right, gives us that inner peace about how we perceive self, and how we treat others with dignity and respect. I suggest that these are things that parents must teach their children in the role of a trainer.

Parent tool for Training: Consistent and proper use of discipline

Parents are Coaches on the Field of Life. Time Frame: Five to twelve years old.

Our role and goal as "Coaches" of our children is three-fold: preparation for separation and infiltration, not isolation. Allow me to explain.

Life is a process of separation: separation from the womb, separation from the home, separation in marriage, and eventually, separation in death. In other words, we are not raising our children to live with us for the rest of their lives. Rather, our job as parents is to prepare them to leave home one day and establish their own life, their own home, and their own family.

This is why I call this phase of parenting "Coaching" because at this stage of life our children are leaving home every day and *playing in the game of life*. They are in school for eight hours a day, five days a week, and nine months a year for the next twelve years (give or take). After high school maybe they will go off to college or get a job. After that, perhaps marriage or some other venture in business, travel, or what have you.

Thus, at this point, we are now like coaches standing on the sidelines watching our children play in the game of life.

We aren't in control of their every move, word, actions, or choices. We are more removed from them and all that we nurtured, trained, and prepared them for will be manifest as they encounter different people in all types of different situations and circumstances.

Secondly, because of the preparation of our children, we can be confident about sending them into the community every day to *infiltrate* the darkness, the temptations, the peer pressure, the toxic environment around them, as an infiltrating light. As an example. As a leader for their peers to follow.

Many parents are afraid of their environment, and rightfully so. They have seen how it can affect children. Too many of their own children have become casualties of their environment with all the risky and toxic elements of drugs, alcohol abuse, gangs, violence, and other negative influences. And yet, if we live in such an environment, it can't be avoided and trying to remove or isolate our children from the reality of our environment is not the answer either.

A huge turning point in the field of medicine happened when physicians discovered that building up the human immune system was the answer to physical health, instead of working to try and rid the environment of all the toxic elements. In POM, I encourage parents to see themselves as the *inoculation* that builds the social immune system of their child that fights off the negative toxins in their social environment. This inoculation is a metaphor for building the integrity of a child. Their respect for self and others and their character. Again, this is why these phases of parenting;

nurturing, training, discipline, and coaching are vital to the health of our children. We cannot remove these negative elements from the environment and isolating our children from them will only weaken their social immune system. As doctors discovered many years ago, a child's immune system is not fully developed at birth and the only way it can get stronger is for the child to get sick so the immune system can develop the antibodies that prohibit the sickness next time.

The Parent as a Coach

I enjoy coaching. I enjoy it because it is a very rewarding experience to help someone improve their performance. Their career. Their life.

Coaching is an act of service. It is servant-leadership in action because you are not the principal person performing. You are not the person the fans are coming to watch in the game. Nevertheless, you are a key person behind the scenes. You are the guide. A resource. You are the person providing the knowledge and discipline that elevates performance to a higher level. That is what coaching is all about. As I like to share about the difference between teaching and coaching: "Not all good teachers are good coaches. But all good coaches are good teachers." What I mean by this is that good teachers have knowledge of the game and can share or explain the formations, strategies, and plays of a game. But that doesn't mean they have improved a player's game performance. That requires good coaching in addition to good teaching. Good coaching takes teaching a step further by showing the players not only the knowledge of the game, but also how to execute the strategies and plays at a superior level. By their knowledge, insights, and instruction of specific drills to practice repeatedly, they improve the players skill level in the game, not just their knowledge of the game.

This is what parent coaching is all about. We are in a very influential position. Parent coaching comes with a lot of responsibility. And because you have nurtured and disciplined your children, they trust you. They listen to you. They believe in your instruction and guidance to improve their performance and achieve peak performance in the game of life.

Parent coaching tools of preparation for separation and infiltration:

- Guide your child to discover and then develop who they really are, not who their peers, rap songs, television programs, and social media say they are. Be an encourager of their personal dreams and visions.
- Encourage the development of their uniqueness. Emphasize they are one-of-a-kind. We are not comparing our child to him, her, or them.
- Be a role model by showing your children how you use your unique gifts and talents to benefit others.

The importance of these time frames for child development cannot be overlooked in terms of preparing children for choosing either a negative or a healthy lifestyle.

CHAPTER TWELVE
Discipline with Love and Fairness
Avoiding the Authoritarian Style of Parenting

Before I get into the subject of discipline, allow me to share three different scenarios so you can think through how you would handle each hypothetical situation. The age group I have in mind for these scenarios is elementary school age.

Scenario One

You have warned your small children while eating dinner not to place their glass of milk too close to the edge of the table to avoid tipping it over and spilling or breaking the glass. While eating and having conversation, one child takes a drink of milk and places the glass at the edge of the table. Shortly thereafter, he is asked to pass the bread. As he reaches to pass the bread, he knocks over the glass, which falls to the floor, spills the milk, and breaks the glass. What would you do? How would you handle this situation?

Scenario Two

You gave your child specific instructions not to stay after school to play and to come straight home so you can pick him up for a dentist appointment. Upon arriving home, your child is not there. You proceed to the school and there he is playing. You ask why he did not go straight home as instructed, to which he replies, *I just forgot.* You tell him he is grounded and proceed to the dentist. When you arrive, the receptionist tells you that your appointment was yesterday. Your child looks at you and says, *I guess you just forgot, Mom* and then wants to know if he is still grounded. How would you handle this situation? What is your answer to your child's question?

Scenario Three

Your child comes home from school with another of several bad reports of behavior in the classroom. You have disciplined her each time, met with the teacher and principal more than once, warned her, and done everything to try and correct the problem. Now what would you do?

The point with these hypothetical situations is not necessarily what is the right thing to do or the wrong thing, but more a matter of stopping to think about your response (as opposed to reacting as we talked about in the personal growth principles) given the time, place, personality of the child, and a host of other things that may have been going on before the situation came about. With that in mind, here are a few observations to consider:

- **Scenario One**—This scenario is to depict a mistake. The question is, should we discipline children for mistakes? In my view, no. I suggest that mistakes provide good opportunities for a teachable moment.

In my experience with my children, this was the type of thing that would cause me to react in anger, yelling, and provoking my child to tears. As a young dad, I wasn't thinking about, nor did I know anything about, *teachable moments*. I just reacted to the fact that my child didn't listen to me, and now we have a broken glass and spilled milk to clean up. Of course, as I grew in my emotional maturity, I later learned how not to react in anger to child mistakes and use the opportunity as a teachable moment by cleaning up the mess together, to give my small children a plastic glass to drink from and remind my child why daddy is asking them not to put their drink to close to the edge of the table.

- **Scenario Two**–This scenario is to depict open defiance of authority. The question is, should we discipline children for open defiance? Answer: In my view, other than extenuating circumstances, yes, there should be consequences for open defiance regardless of the mistake of the parent.

This is a situation where a parent needs to discern if their child really forgot or if they are simply being defiant. It is possible that a child could forget about going straight home because of a dentist appointment. And in that case, a parent might decide that *this time* there won't be any consequences. But if it keeps happening in other circumstances and the child continues to forget, that is usually a matter of defiance to authority. However, in general, whether the child forgot or not, I would still enforce consequences and explain that I have consequences too for my forgetfulness; I'll need to reschedule, take another day and time off work, possibly pay a fee for not showing up, etc. I'd also add that consequences for open defiance would carry much more weight than consequences for being forgetful.

When I share these scenarios in the POM class, this second scenario always generates the most discussion and differing opinions about whether or not there should be consequences for the child who forgot to go home as instructed.

- **Scenario Three**–This scenario depicted two possible situations. First, it could be *a testing of will*, and who's in control. The second possibility is this kind of continuing behavior can be an indicator that something deeper is bothering the child and could be a cry for help. This is why we must be sensitive and attentive to detail with each child and understand the need for discretion in dealing with an ongoing problem. Having said that, sometimes it is simply a battle of *wills* and parents must ultimately win that battle!

Of the three, this is usually the most emotionally draining on parents, and in particular stepparents, if it is their stepchild always getting in trouble. This constant pressure tends to cause many parents to give in to the short-term battle and lose sight of the long-term effects of giving up on trying to correct this constant troubled behavior.

If this is a case of a stubborn, rebellious child refusing to behave, I offer the following long-term strategy as one solution.

First, don't be too hard on yourself. Being a good parent/stepparent doesn't automatically mean our child will be obedient with us and other authority figures. For the most part, I believe if we are doing our best and continue to grow and work on our emotional maturity, as suggested earlier, our stubborn, rebellious child will get it together over time.

Secondly, I encourage parents in addition to their role as a gardeners, trainers, and coaches, to add the role of a farmers. We all know that farming is hard work and basically entails plowing, planting, watering, and cultivating season after season. We also understand that no farmer expects a harvest overnight. Although farming is long, hard work, the harvest will come if we persist with patience. The hope this gives parents dealing with this tough situation is knowing that the law of the harvest is on their side. You will eventually reap what you sow.

Here's how I breakdown this metaphor of the parent as a farmer:

Plowing = Confrontation of the heart

Just as plowing serves the purpose of breaking up the fallow ground to prepare it for the seed, confronting our child's wrong behavior is educating and speaking to their heart and conscience to not allow their hard-heartedness to win them over in the long run. They know what they are doing is wrong. Their mind may be rationalizing their behavior, but their conscience is not in agreement with their emotions or their rationalization. Thus, by confronting their rebellious behavior, we are strengthening the voice of their conscience. The importance of this *plowing the conscience* cannot be overlooked.

Confronting our child on a consistent basis is emotionally exhausting and many parents/stepparents end up losing this battle because they get worn down. It does require the courage to speak up again and again and oftentimes can turn into a heated argument. Nobody gets this right all the time (I know I haven't). It's just the nature of the situation. Nevertheless, what is important to remember is that you come from a place of unconditional love and want to send your rebellious child the message that you believe in them even though you are confronting their unacceptable behavior.

Planting = The seeds we plant are the words we speak

We know words can be a powerful force for good or bad. As mentioned earlier, the old adage "Sticks and stones can break my bones, but words can never hurt me" is probably one of the biggest misconceptions about the power of words and the effect they have on our hearts and minds. The fact is that words matter, especially the words parents use when dealing with a tough situation in the heat of the moment.

When we are upset, it is very easy to say the wrong things and/or say the right things in a wrong way. We can say things we don't mean. We can say things that are mean. Things that belittle, shame, and cause resentment and anger in our children. I cringe to think about all the times I have slipped into this argumentative, angry mode of dealing with rebellion, defiance, and disrespect. Nevertheless, I know what to do when that happens as I discussed earlier, admitting when we are wrong and apologizing, which helps earn respect for your parental authority.

Obviously, raising a blended family of children has provided me a lot of experience with these things and I'm happy to say that I've grown throughout the years and gotten much better at practicing the principles I am sharing in this book. There are a few phrases and words I've learned to use that help me to say a negative thing in a positive way. I encourage you to consider adopting these words (or similar ones you come up with on your own) the next time you find yourself plowing and planting:

- *This is not who you really are.*
- *You're better than this.*
- *I believe in you, but I am not going to accept this behavior from you.*
- *I love you, but I don't love the way you are acting and treating your mother.*
- *I'm on your side and I'm on you again because I love you and I'm trying to help you.*

Watering = Verbal Affirmation

During the farming phase of parenting, it is important to find any time, any opportunity to give verbal affirmation, compliments, and praise for good works and/or any kind of cooperation. Our rebellious child is not the enemy (though it sure does feel like it at times) and we can communicate this message by affirming good behavior for whatever reason, no matter how small a thing it might seem to be.

Cultivating = Affection

This can be hard to do during a time when you are confronting, arguing, frustrated, and emotionally burned out. Actually, I take it back . . . it is darn hard to do in these times. I can remember times when I would just let things go because I was too emotionally exhausted and didn't have it in me to be genuine in making any effort to do any of the above suggestions. I would separate myself from the room or the house and just chill out for a while. I would take the time I needed to regroup and catch my emotional and psychological breath. I would need to have a pep-talk with myself because I knew I couldn't give in and give up the fight for winning back my child (stepchild in this particular case).

At times I had to admit that what I was doing wasn't working, and I needed to check myself and be honest about where I was being a part of the problem. I needed to read, study, and practice my personal and emotional growth principles. It was during these times that I developed different *seeds* to plant so I could expect a different harvest and that is exactly what happened and continues to happen as of this writing.

If you find yourself in this *farming* role let me encourage you here. Don't give in to your emotions and don't give up on your child/stepchild. Keep plowing, planting, watering, and cultivating your own heart and that of your child. The law of the harvest is a real thing, and it is our best hope for winning back our rebellious *prodigal* son/daughter as it were. Persist. Pray. And be patient for your harvest. Although it does not come overnight, it does come. It will come.

The Controversy of Discipline

How to go about disciplining children to teach them respect for parental authority is controversial business these days. Each family will have to determine what form of discipline works best for them.

Many parents struggle between being:

- Too permissive
- Too strict
- Whether to spank or not

In his book, *Dare to Discipline*, the renowned child psychologist, Dr. James Dobson, talks about the *"strong-willed child"* and the need for parents to learn how to *"bend the child's will without breaking their spirit."*[1]

I call this the skill of *just enough*. Think of a musician who must always be fine-tuning their instrument each time they play it. With a guitar, if the musician pulls the string too hard, it will break. If he does not pull it tight enough, it will be out of tune. This skill of just enough is what a parent must learn in the use of discipline.

Common principles for exercising discipline include:

Removing privileges that a child enjoys–Children learn the difference between *rights* and *privileges*. Parents sometimes get these two confused or allow their children to confuse the difference between what is a right and what is a privilege.

For example, do children have the right to have a cell phone? Expect parents to buy them designer clothes? Have complete privacy in their bedroom? My answer to these three questions is No. Thus, as a parent I have the right to remove or disallow these things because they are privileges. Privileges I am allowing my children to have and when I remove them, I am using that as a form of discipline for one reason or another.

Many children are under the impression that their cell phone is *theirs* and a parent has no right to take it away from them. They might even use the argument that they are paying for it. That may be true, but that's beside the point. If my minor's phone is affecting them in a negative way, such as being a distraction from school and chores, causing sneakiness and a lack of communication at home, etc., then I, as a parent, may exercise my authority to take the phone away.

As another example, some children think that their room is their private property and that a parent has no right to invade their privacy. Once again, if my child's room becomes a dark, sneaky, and loud place causing disconnection from the rest of the family, a parent has every right to enter the room to find out what is going on or what is being hidden and causing the disconnection in relationship.

Of course, children do have rights, which include (amongst other things) the right to eat, be sheltered, clothed, and be cared for in love and safety. They have the right to speak up and seek outside help if they are being neglected or abused in any way. They have the right to an education, physical recreation, and social interaction in their neighborhoods, schools, and with friends and extended family, to name a few.

> **Isolation through timeouts**–Isolation can be effective as a form of discipline. I think this is one of those things that works well with small children but maybe not so well with kids as they get older. If a parent chooses to use timeouts, I suggest you choose the appropriate place, sending a kid to their room might be more fun than discipline.

When I used this form of discipline when my children were little, I would take a chair and make them sit facing the wall with nothing to do or look at but the paint on the wall. I would say, "You sit here and think about what you did (or said)." When you're ready to change your attitude and apologize, let me know. It didn't take too long before I got the attitude change and apology needed.

> **Verbal reprimand**–Scolding, reasoning, and lecturing can work if used correctly. By correctly, I mean not used too often or every time we discipline our children. This was always a challenge for me because I am a teacher/coach by nature

and lecturing (yelling) would just burst out of me. However, after I got older and matured as a father, I could see that lecturing and scolding was having a negative effect and causing shame and sadness in my children.

On the other hand, sometimes a scolding and/or lecture can be effective in discipline when spoken with the right degree of seriousness, sincerity, and love.

The True Definition of the Term "Discipline"

To give us more insight and understanding about discipline, let's look deeper into the root definition of the word. The term "discipline" comes from the Latin word *disciplinare*, which means *to teach*. Many people, however, associate the word with punishment, which falls short of the full meaning of the word.

Lessons from a Speech Given by a Major in World War I to Officers in Training

While reading a book on leadership, I came across a story that serves as a powerful analogy for teaching parents the difference between punishment and the true purpose of discipline. In this example, a military officer was training young men to become leaders. He explained that it's unwise to treat everyone the same—what works as discipline for one person may have an entirely different effect on another. He emphasized that a company commander who applies the same standard punishment to all for a given offense is being lazy. Instead, a good leader should study the unique personalities of their men as carefully as a surgeon examines a difficult case. He emphasized that the application or purpose of surgery was to effect a cure, not merely to watch your men *squirm*.

I found this to be a valuable lesson for parents. Just as leaders tailor their approach to the individuals they lead, parents must recognize that the same form of discipline may not be equally effective for every child or stepchild. Understanding each child's personality allows parents to apply discipline that fosters growth and character development rather than merely serving as punishment with no deeper lesson.

Wisdom in Discipline:

- The question we must keep before us when disciplining children is: Will my child learn and want to do better from what I'm going to do? This, of course, requires emotional maturity. The capacity to stop, think, consider, and choose to respond to misbehavior, instead of reacting out of anger, is the key, albeit easier said than done.
- There are times for being firm and there are times when mercy and understanding are called for, and the wise parent knows the difference.

I think this type of discretion by a parent from time to time is not only wise but also goes a long way in establishing respect for your authority and a healthy acceptance of discipline in the future.

Insights from Private Conversations With Rebellious Youth

As mentioned earlier, discipline can be controversial. Many parents take offense when others, like extended family, schoolteachers, coaches, counselors, psychologists, mental health experts, etc., offer their unsolicited advice and opinions about how parents are disciplining their children. And even though it's all well intended, parents have a hard time hearing a message that is basically telling them they need to do a better job in discipling their children.

The voice, however, that is often missing from giving parents feedback on their disciplinary ways is from those on the receiving end of the discipline, children.

As a school counselor, I had the unique opportunity to hear and listen to that voice. Here are some of the common themes I heard:

- We never discuss anything after we have a confrontation.
- Many troubled youths believe their parents/stepparents love their younger or *good* siblings more.
- Too many get the message they are no longer wanted at home or valued as an important member of the family.
- Many felt their parents were guilty of making bad choices in how they handled the wrong behavior of their children but would not admit it.
- And perhaps the most egregious response was the fact

that most parents *never* admit when they are wrong or apologize.

What stood out to me from these conversations—both with students and later with their parents—was how often miscommunication leads to misunderstanding, which is at the heart of many broken parent-child relationships. The key lesson here is that we shouldn't let our children's minds be the sole interpreters of our actions and decisions regarding discipline. More often than not, they perceive the situation very differently than we do.

To prevent these misinterpretations, it's essential to have a conversation once emotions have settled. Explain why you chose to discipline them, listen to their perspective, and, if necessary, apologize. Always bring closure with an affirming hug and words of love and encouragement, reinforcing that discipline is rooted in care, not punishment.

Discipline and the Two Biggest Mistakes Parents of Young Children Can Make

- Not teaching small children to accept *no* for an answer.
- Not teaching small children to accept a *no* answer without an *attitude*.

These are two common parenting mistakes that often get overlooked. As far as I know, most parenting curricula fail to address these crucial child-rearing principles.

One of the most significant lessons children must learn is

how to accept the word *no* from their parents. Unfortunately, when this lesson is not taught, the consequences can be far greater than parents realize. Consider the difference between a teenager who stays out past curfew—exposing themselves to unnecessary risks—and one who comes home on time or doesn't go out at all. Often, the only distinction between the two is obedience to parental authority: one respected the *no*, while the other ignored it.

By teaching children to respect, accept, and obey the word *no*, parents can help them avoid many unnecessary hardships. How many teenagers have faced serious consequences they now regret simply because they refused to accept a parent's authority? Setting firm boundaries and reinforcing them with consistency can protect children from choices they may later wish they had avoided.

On the other hand, while some parents successfully teach their children to accept the word *no*, they often overlook an equally important issue—the negative attitude that can come with it. Ignoring this response is a critical mistake.

I firmly believe that this is a battle parents must address with **consistent, fair, and firm discipline.** Teaching children not only to obey but to do so with a respectful attitude is essential for building strong character and healthy relationships.

Mother Wesley

Susanna Wesley (January 1699 – July 1742) was widely known and respected for her child-rearing principles. As the twentieth of twenty-five children and the mother of 1nineteen of her own, she gained firsthand experience in parenting. Though only eight of her children survived to adulthood, Mother Wesley—as she was affectionately called—remained a model of healthy and effective child-rearing.

Two of her sons, John and Charles Wesley, became renowned for their evangelistic work and were the founders of the Methodist Church. Toward the end of her life, John Wesley asked her to write down her principles on raising children.

Mother Wesley firmly believed in the importance of disciplining children not just for their actions but also for their inner attitudes. She taught that shaping a child's mind begins with guiding their will—transforming stubbornness into obedience. While intellectual development takes time and varies with each child, she insisted that **subduing a child's will should be done as early as possible.** Delaying correction, she warned, would allow stubbornness and disobedience to take root, making it much harder to address as the child grows older.

She strongly criticized permissive parenting, which she saw as mistakenly kind but ultimately harmful. In her view, parents who avoid timely correction in an attempt to *be cool* or indulgent are, in reality, being cruel—because they allow their children to develop habits that will lead to greater hardship and stricter discipline later in life.

Another illustration of this inner attitude is the difference between parents accepting outward compliance but with a reluctant attitude. This reminds me of the story of the father who was trying to control the disorderly and distracting behavior of his child at church who refused to be quiet and sit down during the service. After trying to verbally control his child, but to no avail, the father finally threatened to take his son outside for a spanking if he did not behave. At that, the little boy finally obeyed and sat down. After sitting down, the boy looked at his father defiantly and said, "I might be sitting down on the outside, but on the inside, I am still standing up!"

This is what I'm referring to as a big mistake many parents make by allowing their children to outwardly obey, but neglect to deal with the inner attitude of their reluctant obedience. Outward conformity is not inward respect and obedience. And as disobedient children grow old enough and big enough, our threats and bribes no longer work and they disrespect, defy, and disobey our parental authority. When parents allow, overlook, and ignore this inner defiance of their child, they often end up rewarding it and reinforcing this attitude.

Key Point

Children must be brought into a healthy understanding that outward conformity with an inner attitude of defiance is unacceptable and that consequences are still in force until the inner attitude is transformed into a sincere apology and a rightful respect for authority. Parents will not gain the respect and inward obedience they seek unless they are consistent in bringing consequences for:

- Wrong behavior
- A wrong attitude for the consequences of the wrong behavior.

The BIG "S" Question: What About Spanking?

This issue is very controversial and one I believe deserves to be addressed and discussed in a fair and honest manner. To characterize spanking as a form of violence just isn't accurate. I can agree that such forms of discipline as *caning* and *flogging* are inappropriate forms of child discipline. But to put spanking in that same category is a misrepresentation of how many parents use spanking as a form of discipline. Although it is true that what some parents practice for *the rod of correction* can go overboard and become abusive. We all understand that. However, to paint all parents who spank their children with the broad brush of committing acts of violence and degrading their children is unfair and simply wrong. This is exactly why this issue needs to be discussed in a civil, open-minded manner.

Spanking needs to be properly defined. Spanking is not beating, slapping, punching, kicking, or any other form of physically hurting a child. A spanking is painful, I'll give you that. But it should never be physically abusive and does not need to be psychologically harmful either.

Therapists, psychologists, family counselors, and others will point to a plethora of research and studies to justify their opinions and lend credibility to their argument against spanking. But we have all been subject to research and studies that are false, inaccurate, and biased. What these advocates that support taking away parental authority want is for people like me, who work with parents, youth, and families, to tell parents that they *should not* spank their children for any reason because it is an act of violence that can cause mental and psychological problems in children later in life.

First of all, when exercised properly, I do not believe it is an act of violence. Secondly, it is not my place to take away the right of parents to use proper spanking as a form of discipline should they choose to do so. Thirdly, I believe when spanking is used properly it can be effective as a form of discipline for *some* children. But none of those reasons are my primary purpose for addressing this topic.

My purpose is to keep a promise. A promise I made to the students on my caseload many years ago when I was the at-risk counselor on a school campus.

At that time (early 1990s) I told my students that if they would be honest with me and tell me what was really bothering them and why they were basically destroying their future by the risks and dangerous lifestyle choices they were making, that I would stand up for them. I promised I would come alongside them and speak for them to the school principal, police, or their parents.

This prompted them to open up to me about what was going on behind closed doors. And that prompted me to begin to do home visits.

To be clear, I'm not saying all of them accused their parents of abuse of one kind or another. But some did and that was something I could not ignore legally or emotionally. As I shared earlier on how POM was started, this was one of my primary motivations, as well as the lack of communication, respect, relationship, and overall dysfunction I witnessed during my home visits.

One of the things I discovered was how many parents confuse spanking and/or discipline with physical abuse, and that many parents justify physical abuse in the name of spanking and discipline.

It amazes me how many youth advocates know that children are being improperly spanked and disciplined, yet they refuse to address it and would rather just criminalize parents by calling Child Protective Services without discussing these issues first and making the effort to educate parents that are good people, mean well, and are often just following the discipline practices that they were raised with. Don't get me wrong. Obviously, if real physical abuse is taking place and continues to take place, then by all means the authorities must be called upon to remove a child from such ongoing abuse. That said, in many cases, if parents can be confronted in a spirit of care and empathy, this situation can be corrected without threatening parents with taking away their authority and worse, their children.

For example, one parent told me after completing the POM classes, "I never knew it was wrong to slap my kids. After taking the classes I realized how this was wrong and affecting my relationship with them."

Thus, the POM curriculum does not shy away from this issue, nor take the easy road of criminalizing, disempowering, and shaming parents who spank into believing they are terrible and irresponsible people. Frankly, given the gravity of this issue, I think that is a cowardly way of handling this issue. Shaming, criminalizing parents who spank children, and disempowering parental authority because they are ignorantly disciplining their children is an easy, wrong, and irresponsible non-answer to correct the problem.

To be clear, POM does not advocate spanking, nor make an argument about whether spanking is right or wrong. The important point is: Whether we agree with it or not, or like it or not, many parents do in fact spank their children and that's why we should address it.

In our POM classes, we openly talk about spanking and make the effort to educate parents who spank to strike a wise balance by suggesting several principles for those parents who choose spanking as a form of discipline.

This is my way of keeping my promise. I refuse to remain silent and not speak up for and defend all the physically abused children who have no voice. We can threaten parents and try to legislate this issue away, but it hasn't and won't correct the problem. My experience, after working with and building a trusting relationship with parents, has been a witness to a change of heart and adjustment in disciplinary practices.

The POM curriculum addresses the topic of spanking by offering some guidelines and suggested principles:

- POM does not make an argument for right or wrong on the practice of spanking.
- If parents exercise their right to spank, they should do it properly, but we should not assume that they are doing it properly, which is why we should discuss it.
- We can't expect parents who choose to spank to stop just because others are against it.
- Many parents do not agree with spanking children

for any reason. Many other parents do, in fact, spank their children. Whether we are for it, or against it, both views must be respected.

- Many parents are under the false assumption that it is illegal to spank children. But it is not illegal in the United States. However, there are certain limitations and these need to be clarified.
- What *is* illegal is physically abusing children. Guidance is needed for those parents who do spank to ensure they understand what abuse is and practice discipline through spanking properly.

Suggestion Guidelines: If you choose to spank–be wise and moderate.

1. POM suggests spanking be used as a last resort.
2. Parents should not wait until they are angry before spanking.
3. Parents should explain what behavior the child is being spanked for.
4. Using the hand for one or two swats on the posterior only is sufficient.
5. Parents should talk about the behavior later to bring understanding, reconciliation, and closure.
6. Slapping, punching, kicking, beating and any other form of physical force that is physically harmful to the child is abuse and never acceptable.
7. What is proper spanking? A spank on the posterior– nothing more, nothing less.

8. When should the use of spanking stop? In general, once a child reaches the age of twelve (this is only a suggested guideline and each parent can decide for themselves), other forms of discipline are better suited that recognize the growth and maturity of the child who is beyond the spanking stage.

In the spirit of full disclosure and transparency, I leave you with this thought. I did spank my children as a form of discipline. However, the reason I spanked my children was so I didn't need to spank them. It worked.

CHAPTER THIRTEEN
Community Building– How to Raise Productive Citizens

Community Building in the Home

Building a strong community at home starts with nurturing relationships that cultivate appreciation, respect, care, and joy among family members. For stepparents, prioritizing this investment of time is especially crucial when stepchildren are young, as it lays the foundation for trust and connection.

Family interactions provided on a regular-daily basis can be used to teach children the importance of the following three aspects of community:

Dependence–Small children receive security and a sense of self-worth as their daily needs are tended to by parents. They also need instruction to learn to appreciate the dependence they have on parents to meet their needs. While it is healthy and normal for small children to be attended to by their parents, we should also be attentive to any development of an attitude of entitlement or demanding of parents and/or taking our services to them for granted, which leads me to my next point on teaching independence.

Independence–As our children get a little older, they need to be taught the importance of being able to fend for themselves as an individual expected to be responsible for their own needs. That serves to develop a healthy work ethic that will translate to citizenship that makes a positive contribution to the larger community.

As an example, when your child says, "Mom, I'm hungry."

You respond by saying, "Well, there's some leftovers in the refrigerator you can warm up for yourself."

Or they say, "Mom, all my clothes are dirty."

To which you reply, "Okay, let me show you how to use the washing machine to wash them."

You get the idea. Now, is this being a mean or lazy stepparent? No. We are simply teaching our children to be responsible and tend to their own needs at a level that is very doable for their age.

Inter-dependence–In addition, there needs to be a cultivation of the humility to accept how we need each other to complete the fullness of our life. This is usually a slower process for blended families. As our children grow into their teenage years and beyond, they need some space to discover and grow into their individuality. They want more independence. This is common for all teens and young adults. However, as they get out of the house and explore the world, so to speak, eventually they discover that they still need their parents. They still need their siblings, stepsiblings, extended family, and close friends. In other words, they develop an appreciation for the value of interdependence.

The cycle of moving from dependence to independence and ultimately to interdependence, first learned within the home, mirrors the dynamics of the broader community. As citizens, we are *dependent* upon the essential functions and resources provided by the four foundational institutions of society: government, business, education, and religion. Simultaneously, as individuals, we exercise *independence* as employees and entrepreneurs, working to sustain ourselves and our families. Ultimately, as families, we recognize our *interdependence* with one another; the larger community, forming the fabric of a thriving and diverse community.

Children learn to appreciate and develop family community at home because of parents who:

> **Plan and prioritize a consistent daily schedule.** Eat dinner together without TV, phone calls, texting, or email interruptions. Many families eat dinner together but still allow these distractions that disrupt good conversation that builds family unity and community. Having a set time for dinner might not seem like a big deal, but it is. It provides consistent opportunities for interaction and conversation and prioritizes relationship-building within our immediate family.

Thus, having dinner together is not a time for texting, social media, or anything else that diverts from having a healthy dialogue and eye-to-eye contact with father/stepfather and mother/stepmother. I'm not saying that family dinners are a *guarantee* to winning the loyalty of your stepchildren. However, what I am saying is that parents who plan family dining are making a wise investment and creating an experience for their blended family that will go a long way in winning the battle for loyalty. I can attest to this based on my own personal experience.

Plan and organize fun family activities. These activities can be simple games played at home, outings to the park or beach, or a yearly family vacation. Again, these are special times for building connections and attachments for a lifetime. For that reason, I suggest parents should use discretion when allowing friends or even extended family members to join them because when friends or extended family members are present, it often changes the genuine relational dynamics. Keeping these special times to *just us* allows genuine conversation, blended family camaraderie, stepsibling friendships to deepen, and family traditions and memories to be established.

I'm sure we have all seen how mom or dad *change* when company comes to the house. Suddenly, Dad, who normally has little to say when he comes home from work, becomes the life of the party talking, joking, and laughing. Then the kids wonder and think to themselves: *Gee, Dad, why can't you act like that when it's just us?* Or the reverse might be true. Mom, who normally is the light and life at home talking, laughing, and/or singing, becomes a different person when the in-laws come over or even other adult friends. The same changes in personality happen with the kids as well. The older brother is yelling at or talking down at his little sister or embarrassing his younger brother, wanting to *show off* to his friends. Little sister wants to hang out with her older sister and her friends but is pushed away, which is unusual behavior for her older *best friend* sister. Another thing I've noticed is the forming of *little clicks* that leave others out and causes hurt and jealousy. These situations are intensified when developing a blended family.

You might say that these things are just natural occurrences and are nothing to worry about. Maybe, maybe not. But why rob your children of those special times with *just us*? Why not cultivate a safe environment where we can all get to know each other on a deeper level and not have to worry about putting up a front to impress others outside our immediate family?

Don't misunderstand me. Over the course of time, there were many nights when I did allow or invite the company of my children's friends to have dinner with us. And we had many great times on special outings, parties, and dinners with extended family. I'm not advocating that others should *never* join our family for dinner or vacation. That's taking it too far and not healthy for our children. Nevertheless, it's important for stepparents to be aware of and know how to balance *just us* times with fun activities that do include others in developing an atmosphere of freedom, acceptance, joy, affection, and unconditional love.

I understand that busy schedules can make it feel nearly impossible to carve out time for these special moments. The whirlwind of work, commuting, school, homework, meetings, church, weekend sports, birthday parties, and other events keeps families constantly on the go. It's easy to get caught up in the hustle, leaving little room to simply enjoy each other's company without an agenda or obligations. However, when parents make the effort to intentionally plan these moments, it can be a game changer, especially for blended families helping to build stronger connections and lasting memories.

There are plenty of opportunities right in the city or town where you live. Opportunities to build *just us* time right in your own backyard or even right in your own home. Try it and see what happens.

Insist on a commitment to each other's important activities. Each family member should attend (unless legitimate circumstances don't allow) and support each parent and/or sibling's significant activity, such as school plays, sporting events, awards ceremonies, etc.

My three daughters grew up on the baseball diamond, basketball court, and football fields watching their two older brothers compete. When they grew up and joined their own athletic competition in cheerleading, ballet, and basketball, my boys weren't always keen on going to watch their special *girl* events. But I didn't allow that. They didn't have a choice, but I exercised my authority and insisted that they go. I'd say, "Your sisters attended your games and now it's your turn to support them."

A lot of parents don't do that. And even more sadly, a lot of parents can't do that because their children have lost respect for their authority and are dictating what they will and won't do and where they will and won't go. Why does this matter? It matters because we are building a community. We are teaching the value of support and concern for others, which are values integral to a healthy community.

Monitor the daily dialogue between all family members. We need to have an ear for how our children address each other. There is always room for nicknames and joking with each other in a loving way. I'm not talking about that. I'm talking about unkind words, name-calling, and being mean to one another with words. Children listen to and pick up words from everyone and everywhere. If we are paying attention to the lyrics in the music they listen to, the dialogue on social media, movies we watch, and the language some parents use around other adults, it should come as no surprise when we hear our children parroting these same profane words with each other. The point is, what are we going to do about it? Or is this just another thing to look the other way on and not worry about it? *It's just part of growing up . . . isn't it?* I suppose it is. Yet, I still believe parents can provide proper coaching to instill the values of etiquette, politeness, courtesy, and respect for how we speak to one another beginning in our home.

I understand that when our kids get older, and when they are not at home, they are going to do and say things we might not approve of at home. After all, I did the same thing. But there is one way of talking at home and another way of speaking to friends and in the streets. But what we are talking about here is building citizenship. Building community in the home that will carry forward into the public square. I believe our neighbors, teachers, police, businesses, and employers appreciate young people who present themselves with what back in the day used to be called *having manners*.

One way to do this is to play games together. This allows parents to build sportsmanship and also monitor language used between siblings, correct disrespectful language, teach how to apologize, ask for forgiveness, and receive forgiveness if their competitive nature crosses the line of inappropriate behavior.

Develop family traditions. For example, attending church together, yearly camping, holidays, dinners, etc. As mentioned earlier, I was not raised with any family traditions, so I created my own. I'm suggesting something with you and your children that becomes a yearly *thing* that everyone looks forward to that carries into their adult years and hopefully something they will carry on long after we are gone. Usually, these kinds of traditions can be built around the holidays. That's what we did with our children as they were growing up. But with a little creativity, there are many ways to develop family traditions that become another form of attachment and build family unity and community.

Volunteering for community service together. There are ample opportunities for volunteer service in every community via schools, churches, nonprofit organizations, and the like. Intentionally involving your children in community service in one form or another creates a sense of caring, belonging, and allegiance to things that are bigger than us, which is an important and mature attitude children need to learn from parents as the way good citizens give to and build safe and healthy communities.

More Tips for Raising Good Citizens That Contribute to Healthy and Safe Communities

Below are five principles I encourage parents to use as guidelines for teaching children citizenship and community contribution:

1. Teach children:

- Their life is not an accident.
- They were born on purpose, with a purpose.
- They exist for a reason bigger than just themselves.
- They have a significant role to play in the community.
- That success and significance are found in service to others. Use movies, stories, books, friends, relatives, etc. as examples of people who used their gifts and talents to make great contributions to their community.

2. Tell children:

- Their life is a reward and a blessing, not a burden.
- Write them short letters or notes and express how you feel about them. Send them a card in the mail to

express the positive contributions they make to the family, school, or community.
- When appropriate, ask older siblings or extended family members to do the same.

3. Help children:

- Discover their gifts and talents.
- Get involved in sports, arts, music, and other activities that will bring out their natural talents.
- Help them be who they are. Hide any disappointment you may feel if your son is not the star athlete, or your daughter is not the star dancer you hoped they would be. Be sensitive to the unique development of each individual child. Nobody forms well in someone else's mold.
- Partner with schools and be encouraged to question school officials, school policies, or other aspects of your child's education.

4. Develop Children:

- Invest and expose them to mentors who have accomplished their dreams.
- Coach them to practice and appreciate the discipline that sharpen their skills.
- Participate in community events with your kids to show them how others are using the same talents they have to make a difference in the community.

5. Prepare your children:

- For their destiny in society and the world.
- Use television programs, commercials, news, movies, and music to teach your children how to analyze, think, and learn for themselves.
- As early as possible, give your child the gift of READING. Higher education does not always take place in expensive colleges and universities. Learning to read wide and deep is the key to success for anyone. If you can't provide the above things for your child, find those in the community who can.

CHAPTER FOURTEEN
Reconciliation in Blended Families
The Power of Forgiveness and Unconditional Love

To say that ALL families have problems may be a stretch. I don't know. To be safe, let me say that most, *if* not all, families encounter problems of one kind or another at one time or another. Thus, family problems, as they were, are nothing unusual. Nothing to fear, be surprised by, or unexpected. Different families, such as blended families, experience different kinds of problems in various degrees and circumstances.

These days, we are much more aware of family problems. And for better or worse, we are much more exposed to what in times past would be known as "family secrets." But the issue is not the fact that families have problems. The issue is what we do about them. It's about how we handle them, reconciling differences, family falling-out's, arguments, heated confrontations, and offensive words or actions.

To answer these questions, there is a story I like to use that I believe provides a great example for guidance in the principles of wisdom for handling difficult situations. The story is one many people are familiar with and it is found in the Bible in the Gospel of Luke, Chapter 15, called, *The Prodigal Son*.[1]

I believe whoever titled this story *The Prodigal Son* got it wrong. They missed the point of the story, which is not about the son, but rather it is about what I call, "The Great Father."

The story starts by mentioning *a certain man*. This certain man, with two sons, is what the story is about. If you're not familiar with this story allow me to paraphrase a version of it here:

One day, the younger of the father's two sons comes to his father and declares that he wants to receive all his inheritance *now*. Apparently, he's not happy living at home and working for his father and wants to go out on his own to do his own thing. The father does not argue, grants his son his inheritance, and the son leaves to take a journey to a far country. At some point thereafter the son squanders all his inheritance. He blows it on drink, drugs, prostitutes, and all manner of the party life. Eventually, he finds himself homeless, broke, and starving in a pig pen eating with the pigs. In that tired and broken place, the story says, *he came to himself* and said, *what the heck am I doing here working and eating with pigs? My father has servants who have plenty to eat . . . I could go home* (my paraphrase).

Now, let me pause here and ask you a question. I want you to stop for a moment and consider how many runaways, rebellious youth, are out in the streets right now and possibly have *come to themselves*, because they are tired of being out there on their own, and in that broken condition can truly say, "I could go home?"

It saddens me to say, not many.

You see, the reason the prodigal son could say that is because he knew what kind of father he had. He knew the type of man his farther was. He knew his character. And that is what the story is about. The Great Father. The kind Father. The unconditional loving Father. The wise Father patiently hoping for the return of his lost son.

And so, the son gets up and begins his journey back home. When he is getting closer to home, his father sees his son from afar, and he runs to his son before he reaches home and showers him with hugs and kisses. He does not rigidly stand there with an *I told you so* attitude. Or, the snide remark, *I knew you'd be back*. He doesn't start *shoulding* on him, *you should've never left, You shouldn't have done that, You should've listened to me*, etc. Nor does the father shame him like so many parents do when the wayward son or daughter returns. However, the son, being ashamed of himself, kneels before his father and begins to tell his father he has really screwed up and is no longer worthy of being his son. He does not ask to be taken back as a son, but rather in the lowest rank of a slave. However, the father would have none of that and turns to his servants and tells them to bring the best robe, the family ring to place on his son's finger, and new shoes to wear, and then says, *and bring the fatted calf, kill it and cook it so we can eat and celebrate the return of my lost son!* (my paraphrase)

Let me pause again here and point out a few things that are very significant about the time, place, and culture in which this story is being told.

- Under Jewish law, a father of this stature was not allowed to leave, let alone run, from his property anytime he liked.
- The fact that he saw and ran to his son shows that he apparently had been waiting and watching for his son to return.
- Before the son can finish asking to come home as a servant, the father cuts him off and tells the servants to bring a robe, which at that time and culture stands for honor; the ring signifies authority; the shoes signify the status only a son would receive as slaves did not get to wear shoes because they were a sign of freedom.

But the story does not end there . . .

Now the elder son, who had been working out in the fields, is on his way home and hears music, dancing, laughter, and the sounds of joy. He comes upon one of the servants and asks, "What's happening?"

The servant replies, "Oh, your father is throwing a party!"

"Oh, yeah. Why?"

Again, the servant replies, "The party is to celebrate your brother who has returned home!"

At this the elder son becomes furious! *What? Why that lousy, no good rebellious idiot* (My speculative words), and on and on he goes criticizing his brother. As the elder son expresses his anger, and refusing to go into the party, the father, who is inside enjoying the party, sees his elder son outside having his tantrum. So, what does the father do? Or, better yet, what doesn't he do? He doesn't say, *oh get over yourself.* Or *stop whining and thinking about yourself.* Or *stop acting like a spoiled brat!* No. This is a great Father.

He goes out to his elder son and calmly asks him what's wrong? The son in anger says, "All these years I have been with you faithfully working hard and I have never disobeyed you or done the things like your son who wasted all you gave him. And yet you throw him a party and kill the fatted calf? You never did that for me. You never gave me a calf to celebrate with my friends."

After patiently listening to his elder son's rant, the father explains to him, "Son, everything I own, everything I have is yours and has always been yours. But your brother was lost, spiritually dead, and gone. But now he has awakened and returned to himself and to us and that is something we must rejoice in and celebrate."

This is what the story is about. A Great Father that has:

- Unconditional love for his rebellious son.
- Patience in the heartache of waiting for his son to hopefully reach the hardship of life that would cause him to repent and come back home.
- Emotional maturity of pre-forgiveness. He obviously had already forgiven his son as demonstrated by initiating the reconciliation by running to him and hugging, kissing, receiving, and honoring him as his son and not a servant.

- Generosity in throwing a party by using the fatted calf, which in those days signified wealth.
- Principles of humility, patience, kindness, and forgiveness that demonstrated to the self-righteous, jealous son how to reconcile a broken family relationship.

Blending families is tough work. And though you may not have experienced the exact circumstances of the above story, I submit that the same principles apply when we find ourselves in a strained, estranged, or broken parent/stepparent-child relationship that occurs for one reason or another.

The easy (and I will add dysfunctional) thing to do is to sweep it under the proverbial rug. Ignore the issue or the other person. Not talk about what happened. Take a posture of denial, pride, fear, anxiety, anger, and laziness, all of which are barriers to producing a healthy reconciliation.

We probably all know friends or family members who have suppressed some very deep emotional issues for years. Perhaps you have suppressed some difficult issues yourself. But what we know about suppressed emotions is that they cause depression and/or eventually come out in ugly ways, oftentimes towards innocent people we love and people who love us, and round and round the dysfunctional cycle goes, and the hurts, violations, and deep wounds are never resolved, and trust is never restored.

These are the kinds of challenges I address in POM when working with biological and stepparents, encouraging them to stop avoiding and start confronting their family relationship struggles—beginning with themselves. This is one of the main reasons I wrote this book.

As a stepfather in a blended family, I haven't just observed these struggles; I've lived them. I know firsthand the pain, frustration, anger, and the temptation to give in or give up when facing the unique challenges of stepparenting, remarriage, and the exhausting effort required to build a healthy blended family.

If you've read this far in my book, I hope you have found the challenges, insights, and encouragement to realize what I call the "POM experience." This transformational process is what helps parents/stepparents become willing and ready to initiate the reconciliation process as necessary. Here are a few examples:

> *I want to thank you for a very awesome class. . . I never was a mother to my children. I didn't have the tools or patience to even be one. You have helped me by giving me the tools and motivation to begin this new life. I'm so excited to get out and become a mother to my children. Thank you, Mr. Ramos, for helping me and my children's lives.*
> —Tiffany Lujan

> *They say, like father, like son. My dad was a man of few words, like me. My son sits in a jail cell. I feel I have failed him. I now realize I haven't. I plan to visit him and apologize to him. To tell him I love him, care about him, and will not give up on him.*
> —Jim Compton

I have identified and accepted my mistakes in raising my children. There is no excuse. I can no longer think that being a single parent is a handicap. Now, when I return home, I'm going to tell the kids I'm sorry, you were right, I was wrong, please forgive me for the yelling and not paying attention and spending quality time doing things together.

–Audrey Brass

Hi Richard, I must say my way of thinking and approach to life and parenting has been forever changed by the recent POM training I received. I was familiar with the curriculum but didn't truly "get it" until I went through your leader training. On a personal level I have been able to see where I went wrong and make amends with my daughter and myself. I stopped blaming myself and simply named myself as the parent God created me to be. Thank you so much for this gift. It has taken me a long time to overcome my shame.

–Rhonda Starr

Dear Richard, my wife and I took the Parents on a Mission program two years ago . . . it changed the relationship with our two sons for good.

–Hector Ruvalcaba

This is the essence of parental emotional maturity and leadership—looking inward to recognize how I might be contributing to the challenges I face, whether at work, within my family of origin, in extended relationships, or at home. Depending on the situation, this kind of self-examination can be incredibly difficult. But the rewards of applying the principles of reconciliation are invaluable, bringing healing, connection, and a stronger foundation for the future.

CHAPTER FIFTEEN

How Stepparents Win Loyalty- Leading Your Blended Family to Success

If you take nothing else away from reading this book, PLEASE hear me on this . . . it is the crux . . . the bottom-line . . . the heart and soul of my POM message:

Every parent in America—and likely around the world—must realize that they are in a daily competition for the heart, mind, and loyalty of their children. If you don't recognize this or remain unaware of it, you're not even in the game.

So, mom, dad, stepparents, it's time to step up and get in the game. Because what's at stake is your child's loyalty. And thus, the real question—the challenge—you need to focus on is this: Who will win the battle for their loyalty? Assuming it will automatically be you is a dangerous mistake.

Competition from Public School Policy

The deliberate undermining of parental authority in many public schools today is almost unbelievable. The fact that elected school board members, teachers, and even some judges are actively restricting parents' rights to be involved in their children's education and curriculum is deeply concerning. One of the most troubling and recent policies is the push to encourage children to keep secrets from their parents about life-altering issues they are facing. This not only erodes trust within families but also places children in vulnerable positions without the guidance and support they need most. The excuse and rationale from the school is that this is being done for the sake of the child to protect them from the harm that will come if their parents are told about their personal struggles with something as important as gender identity. What an insult. The audacity of the school to keep parents in the dark about such a major and life-changing issue. But this (amongst other things parents are outraged about) is what is taking place in our day and age of what public education has become.

"Critical pedagogy" is a term that refers to a political point of view regarding how students should be educated. I don't mean to go down a rabbit hole of politics here as that is not the purpose of POM. But, to keep in line with this chapter's subject of loyalty, my purpose is to awaken parents to what is taking place with their children in the public schools. To be fair, if you are aware and in agreement with the philosophical and political position state school boards and legislatures (like here in California) have assumed, then end of discussion. However, like many parents that I have met and spoken to, many parents are not aware of what is taking place within the hearts, minds, and loyalties of their children from a moral values and worldview perspective.

We witnessed this during the COVID-19 pandemic when schools were shut down and children were attending school via ZOOM. This led to parents at home who began to overhear what teachers were saying and teaching protest at school board meetings. Parents were unaware and expressed outrage and disapproval with subject matter they felt was inappropriate for their elementary school children. The issues of sex education and gender identity are front and center as we are all hearing and seeing. To say these are important issues is an understatement. These subjects and realities are loaded with all kinds of opinions and moral questions that parents do not want their children to discuss in the schoolhouse. Parents have not given their consent for teachers, counselors, or other social specialists to teach or discuss these adult topics and inculcate the minds of their children with a point of view that they may not agree with. To think that children need parental consent to receive an aspirin from a school nurse or to go on a field trip with their teacher and classmates but need no parental consent to discuss sex, get an abortion, or decide their gender identity is the height of hypocrisy, and an ethical violation of parental authority and rights. And it does not stop with sex and gender identity but also includes politicizing the hearts and minds of public school children.

Parents are not only being undermined but we are also being betrayed. We cannot count on our institutions to support or honor the values that we choose to live and teach to our own children. It truly is an intentional effort to transfer power away from us. This anti-parent influence is essentially all around us. And with the advancement of technology, the hard fact is there is no escaping it. That's the bad news. But the good news is that there is a way parents can counter its influence which I will address shortly.

The Power of Technology and the "4Ms" in the Heads Down Generation

In addition, we are living in a technological age that we have never experienced before, and it is only going to get more and more intrusive in every aspect of our family, work, education, and community relationships. We are not only being influenced but becoming addicted to it. Take, for example, our smartphones. It seems so many just can't put them down. Can't stop looking at it. Can't get enough of messaging, checking, scrolling, and clicking. I call it the *heads down generation.* Heads down in the car, heads down in the classroom, at the dinner table, in the living room, at the beach, at the airport, on the plane, on the bus, while standing in line, in the restaurant, and in the bedroom for heaven's sake! The same happens with even the youngest of children addicted to their tablets and/or their parents' smartphone looking to be entertained. Here's one teacher's observation of the effect this is having on children in an email I received:

FROM A TEACHER:

Yesterday, I shut down class about five minutes early and told my students I wanted them to just sit and talk to one another. Several of them immediately opened their laptops and began navigating to their favorite computer game.

I said, 'No, no laptops. I want you to have face-to-face conversations right now.'

After a collective groan went up, I observed something both wonderful and alarming. For the next few minutes, a couple of tables came alive with conversation. They looked at each other in the eyes and talked with great enthusiasm and interest. It was beautiful to watch and listen to.

However, many students were deflated. They did not know what to do without some sort of entertainment from a device. A couple of them put their heads down and avoided eye contact with anyone. I went around the room to those students and tried to engage with them. Some of them mustered a few words, but most didn't know what to do.

I share this story as a wakeup call for parents, grandparents, and guardians. It's tragic to me that

> *a large percentage of today's youth do not know how to have real conversations, but it's not their fault. It is our responsibility as adults to lead by example and hold our kids accountable. Unplug every day, talk, and listen to your children. Getting lost in a device does not help them cope with and overcome the things they're going through mentally, emotionally, and spiritually. All it causes is isolation and depression. They need relationships; they need you.*

The 4Ms

In general, your competition comes from four sources that I call the 4Ms:

- Music
- Movies
- Magazines
- Media

None of us can escape this constant bombardment of 24/7/365 noise, news, and nuisance. That's not to say that I don't enjoy music, watching movies, listening to the news, or using social media. That's not my point. The issue is the messaging and the mesmerizing that is interfering with our relationships and ability to have a simple conversation with our children.

Have you ever thought about the message of the music your kids listen to constantly? Many parents have no idea of the lyrics to the songs their kids listen to. What types of movies are your kids watching? And what is the message your children are being influenced by? The same goes for the messaging from regular TV programs that many parents are put off by, but that are socially normalizing our children. And with today's access to the internet via computers and social media via smartphones, the negative influences have become all too obvious.

In their book, *The Violence Project–How to Stop a Mass Shooting Epidemic*, Jillian Peterson and James Densley found that because of the influence of social media on teens their number one goal for success is to become famous by the number of likes they receive from their followers and how many followers imitate them on social media platforms like Tik Tok.[1]

Again, this is not to say that all uses of social media are bad. And I am not advocating that parents remove or disallow all uses of music, movies, and social media from their children. As a matter of fact, that would probably be counterproductive. The parental message I am advocating here is not about abstention from, but about awareness of the daily competition we face and to get in the game!

Lessons on Loyalty from A Teenage Gang Member

Youth street gangs in certain geographic areas of the country are one of many negative lifestyle choices parents worry about with raising children in a gang culture neighborhood or school environment. Growing up in this environment myself, I know of the temptation and pressure to fit in, be cool, belong, and *be down* as the saying goes.

Being in a gang is all about loyalty. That's the mentality: loyalty to your homeboys and loyalty to your hood. That's what you are committing yourself to when you decide to join a street gang. But the question this begs is why? Why does a young girl or a young boy make this kind of choice? As it turns out the answer is quite simple as expressed by this fourteen-year-old girl gang member in her own words and exactly as she wrote it:

> EVERYONE WANTS TO KNOW WHY. WHY DID YOU JOIN? YOU HAVE A FAMILY WHO LOVES AND CARES FOR YOU. WHY MIJA, WHY? I JOINED BECAUSE WHEN I WAS A LIL GURL ALOT SHYT HAPPENED TO ME THAT NOBODY KNOWS ABOUT AND I HAVE KEPT INSIDE OF ME ALL THYZ TYME. NOWBODY LISTENED TO ME AND WHEN THEY DID, THEY SAID I WAS LYING. DRUG ADDICT DAD AND WORK ALCOHOLIC MOM, NO BROTHERS, NO SISTERS, A STEPDAD THAT ONLY WANTS TO TOUCH ME. AND A BABYSITER WHOSE SON DID TOUCH ME. MY MOM ALWAYS RIPPING ME OUT OF FAMILIES THAT I THOUGHT WERE MINE, IT WAS ALL LIES.
> LIVING IN THA GHETTO WONDERING

> WHY? CAN YOU TELL ME WHY? CAN YOU TELL ME WHY I WAS BORN IN THIS LIFE OF SEX DRUGS AND ALCOHOL, BACKSTABBING OF MY SO CALLED REAL FAMILY? I WAS JUST A LIL GURL DANM. THOSE MEMORIES ARE WITH ME FOREVER I'M SCARED TO LIVE LIFE I'M SCARED TO TRUST N-E BODY, I'M SCARED.
>
> SO WHY DID I JOIN? I JOINED BECAUSE I NEEDED SUMONE AND THEY WERE THE ONLY ONES THERE. I NEEDED SUMONE TO MAKE ME FEEL WANTED AND I NEEDED SUMONE TO CARE. THAT'S WHY.

Here in her testimony, this young girl answers the three questions that have eluded scholars, community authorities, and law enforcement at the federal, state, and local levels: 1) What is a gang? 2) Why do kids join gangs? 3) What is the best method of preventing kids from joining gangs?

This young lady simply tells us that: 1) A gang is a replacement for the family, 2) The reason kids join gangs is because they can't trust their own family to be loyal to them, and 3) The best method for preventing kids from joining gangs is to help parents be better parents.

It's just that simple and does not require millions of dollars for more studies, more laws, more school rules, or more police on the street to figure this out. In addition to the above three answers, she also offers some important lessons and insights regarding family relationships and loyalty:

- Family instability breeds insecurity and confusion.

- Violated personal trust causes suppressed secrets that breed disloyalty.
- Children who don't feel they belong feel scared and alone.
- Children who have no sense of being respected feel silenced.
- Children given no value feel cheap.
- Children given no family purpose will look for one somewhere else.
- Dysfunctional families cause misplaced trust.
- A decision of misplaced loyalty is an issue of trust lost by the family.
- Kids give away their loyalty as a second choice, not as their first choice.
- Initially, every child desires to give their loyalty to their parents, but parents must be willing to pay the price to win/earn it.
- When parents win the loyalty of their children, it gives them the strength to say "no" to peer pressure because their peers are asking for a loyalty already given away to their first family.
- Parents are competing every day in many ways for the loyalty of their children and the best way to win this competition is to build relationships of trust.

From my perspective, communities have been asking the wrong question that has led to taking the wrong approach in addressing youth and local street gangs. The question should not be, *why do kids join gangs* . . . but rather, *why do most kids not join gangs?* And the answer is that the reason most kids don't join gangs is due to the type of family culture they are raised in and their strong and healthy relationship with their parents.

Therefore, the best *prevention* strategy communities can invest in is emphasizing, supporting, and strengthening parental authority and leadership in the home, rather than what many schools, media, and government are doing these days to undermine parental authority and influence with their children away from their parents and their family values as I have outlined here and above.

So, how can parents defeat their competition from the undermining of schools, the influence of social media, the 4Ms, and gangs, and win the loyalty of their children? In POM, we share four very simple methods.

1. Family History, Tradition, and Legacy

The key factor in developing loyalty is to meet the basic human need to belong. As social beings, we all have this innate desire to be a part of something meaningful. A desire to find our place in the world. A desire to pledge our loyalty to something bigger than ourselves. A desire to belong. Our family of origin is the first place we seek to fulfill this need for rootedness, attachment, and connectedness to help us gain an understanding of the world.

Below is an exercise I use to help parents think about their family history, traditions, and legacy. I explain that this is an exercise that requires time for reflection and should not be completed in class. I am simply introducing the idea as one way to inspire them to give deep thought to describing their family: Who are we? What is our family about? What matters to us? And more importantly, what do we want our family legacy to be for our children and grandchildren? If parents have children from ten years old and up, I encourage them to include their children in developing their family legacy. This serves as a powerful way to engage children in anchoring their heart to a cause, a purpose, and to be proud of their family heritage and history.

As you see in the illustration below, I ask the parents to use their last name as an acronym along the left-hand side of the paper. Each letter in their last name is used to describe who their family is and what their legacy is about. If they have multiple last names or have been divorced, etc. I instruct them to decide which last name they feel will best be useful for describing their family legacy.

Family Legacy Exercise
Family History, Tradition, and Legacy

> Revolutionary
> Advocate
> Mission
> Original
> Spiritual

This may seem like a simple tool, but I have seen many families take this exercise to heart with their children and come away with a very positive experience that moves them closer to attachment, winning, and earning the loyalty of their children.

2. The Family Mission Statement

A second tool I suggest to parents for winning loyalty is the creation of a family mission statement (In your case it will be a stepfamily or blended family mission statement like mine). I learned the value of this many years ago from one of my book mentors, Stephen R. Covey (Book mentors are those people I never personally met, but whose writing and courses mentored me as a student of their teaching). Developing a family mission statement with your children is one of the best leadership activities parents can use to give their children a sense of belonging, value, purpose, and guidance for their lives.

This probably seems like the same thing as the legacy exercise I previously shared. However, there is a distinct difference: The legacy exercise is about a long-term vision. Its focus is the future and something we want to pass on from generation to generation. The mission statement is more about right now that serves to provide guidance on a daily basis towards specific values, roles and goals, and the priorities and principles to practice for achieving our goals.

How to Develop a Blended Family Mission Statement

There are four basic steps in this process. However, you may decide on a different process for your family. That's fine. You know what will work best with your family. You might be in a situation where your stepkids are still very young—maybe too young to participate in this first iteration of your mission as a family. Or perhaps you feel they are not ready to have this type of discussion yet. It may be too early in your relationship as a stepparent and so waiting is the wise thing for now. Or maybe you're hearing this for the first time and your children/stepchildren are adults and no longer living at home. There are any number of different family situations you could be in, but the important thing is you see the value of taking a more formal approach of coming together as a family to discuss and develop a mission that speaks to all your blended family members. Remember, your purpose is to win the hearts, minds, and loyalty of your children.

Step 1. Plan a day to gather your family on a day, time, and place with no distractions. Give your children a heads-up at least a few days beforehand so they won't make any plans for that day and time. It's not a good idea to tell them a day ahead of time or the morning of the meeting. For example: Let's say the best time for your family would be on a Saturday morning. You then let them know on Tuesday or Wednesday that you want to have an hour of their time to talk about an idea you learned about developing a family mission statement and you would like to begin the process on Saturday. The goal here is to get a commitment of day and time.

Step 2. On that Saturday morning you briefly explain what a family mission statement is, its purpose, and why you think it's a good thing for your family. Before proceeding to start developing the mission statement, you ask if they have any questions or comments. Once everyone has had a chance to speak (depending on your stepchildren's age, they may have nothing to say at this point, or a lot to say. No worries or hurries.)

Now you're ready to lead the discussion (if your wife or significant other, or one of your children are able, someone needs to take notes) by asking for input to questions like the following (These are only suggestions. You don't have to ask them all necessarily):

- What is the purpose of our family?
- What are we best at as a family?
- What kind of family do we want to be?
- What kind of home do we want people to find when they visit us?
- What are the things we feel are most important to our family?
- What are our highest priorities and goals?
- What are our unique talents and gifts we can contribute to others?
- What values do we want to live by (honesty, fairness, trust, etc.)
- What are our responsibilities to our neighborhood and community?

Step 3. Based on the input from all family members to the questions above, designate someone (usually a parent) to take time after your meeting and begin to write a first draft of your mission statement.
- Try to combine everyone's thoughts.
- Ask for help with the wording if needed.
- Use your imagination–don't worry about length or format at this point.

Basic characteristics of the mission statement:
- Includes characteristics of family culture (loving, kind, giving, etc.)
- Speaks to the effect of the mission statement upon the family (stronger, more spiritual, patient, etc.)
- States a meaningful purpose (to serve the community, etc.)
- Identifies a family's source of strength (faith, integrity, principles, etc.)

Step 4. Call another family meeting (Don't wait too long or you'll lose any excitement or momentum you created in the first meeting). Share the first draft to get feedback and any suggestions for edits or corrections. Work on the final draft together until everyone is satisfied with the wording of the final version.

Step 5. (Optional) This is a chance for your or your children's creativity. How do you want to display the family mission statement? Do you want to make it into a nicely lettered graphic design and frame it to display on a wall in your home? Do you want to print it on a business card with a family logo to give to each of your children to carry with them? Do you want to create a digital version you can all put on your phones?

There are a lot of options, but the main thing is to find a way to put the mission statement in front of your children. Give it significance. Read it together and most of all live it together.

Sample Family Mission Statements:

"The mission of our family is to create a nurturing place of order, truth, love, happiness, and relaxation, and to provide opportunities for each person to become responsibly independent and effectively interdependent in order to achieve worthwhile purposes."

> "Our family mission is to love each other . . . To help each other . . .
> To believe in each other . . . To wisely use our time, talents, and resources to bless others . . . To worship together . . . Forever."

The Ramos/Gonzalez Family Mission Statement:

- Establish a positive influence in the community through our example of love for God and one another.
- Build fun, honest, and trusting relationships through quality time and communication with each other.
- Support one another with respect, participation, understanding, and forgiveness.
- Develop an open, relaxing, clean, and beautiful home that everyone is drawn to.
- Inspire one another to set goals that help us reach our God-given potential individually and as a family.

3. The Power of High Touch in a High-Tech World

Another tool we teach in POM is what I call the power of "High Touch." When was the last time you sat down and hand wrote a letter? A time invested in careful thought about how you wanted to express your feelings, your heartfelt emotions, possibly re-writing it until you have expressed yourself with just the right words. And the reason that we invest this focused time to write is because intuitively we know that words have power.

In today's high-tech world, we have become accustomed to communicating via the convenience of texting and email. Nothing is wrong with that. However, there is still something special . . . something deeper and a little more powerful about handwritten words. If you have ever written a poem, a song, or a love letter, you know what I mean. It takes focused concentration for an extended period of time. That's because to write a short meaningful letter requires a lot of time for thoughtfulness.

This tool, I believe, is another effective way to win loyalty. It may seem simplistic but that short (or long) handwritten note your child finds in their lunch bag or sports bag or receives in the mail can go a long way in building trust and winning the heart, mind, and loyalty of your child.

My five children were all very athletically inclined when they were growing up. That allowed me the opportunity to write a short letter or note to them and then stick it in their helmet, baseball or basketball shoes, ballet shoes, or cheerleading bag. In that letter I would encourage them on their performance and assure them that their mom and I would be watching and cheering them on. I know they appreciated that gesture and it did (and still does) help build our relationship. These days, we still practice the handwritten words with each other in cards on birthdays, holidays, and special occasions, expressing ourselves in writing in addition to the words that are already in the store-bought card. I know how much their words mean to me and I'm sure they feel the same way about my handwritten words to them.

These kinds of things, expressing our love and appreciation, never get old. They never become unnecessary or undervalued. We are social beings with physical, emotional, psychological, and spiritual needs. Parents should not undervalue their role in meeting these needs for their children regardless of their age, distance, or because of a strained relationship due to an argument or something else that may hold you back from reaching out in this manner if needed.

1. The Secret Prevention Weapon Hidden in Every Home

A fourth suggestion we make regarding winning loyalty is encouraging parent heroes in the home. I call it "the secret prevention weapon hidden in every home" because I believe children who look up to their parents as heroes *almost* always choose loyalty to family over choosing loyalty to negative influences and lifestyles.

Definition of a Hero:

- A Hero is someone bigger than life
- Someone to look up to
- Someone who is what I want to be
- Someone who does great things to help others
- Someone who I can trust and depend upon to always be there when I need them
- Someone who is loved by all

With this definition, we have just described Superman/woman, but that is what a hero is in a sense. An almost mythical, mystery kind of a person, beyond the ordinary, unlike the rest of us, or so we think anyway, and somehow it almost doesn't matter whether it is true or not or whether they really exist or not, because we can still draw inspiration from this figure we have in our heart and mind as a personal source of inspiration.

Of course, our children will also draw inspiration from other heroes they may have such as Rock Stars, Movie Stars, and Sports Stars. That is common and nothing to necessarily worry about. But my point here is to inspire moms and dads to see themselves as heroes as well and have a desire to ultimately be the main hero in the lives of their children as they grow older.

At this point, I hope you are saying to yourself and asking yourself: *Okay, Richard. I want to be the hero of my children . . . how do I do that?* I'm glad you asked.

I suppose there are a lot of ways to be a parent hero. However, I'm not trying to make this difficult with an exhaustive list of credentials or qualifying attributes for being a hero. What I share in POM are three very basic principles that any parent can do.

Priorities. As adults we choose our priorities. Part of being a hero to our children is the consistent choice of investing time in our children's activities as first, important, and top priority.

I believe our children understand that because of work and other responsibilities we may have that we can't always make every event they are involved in. Nevertheless, we consistently and gladly participate as much as possible to be supportive and show our interest and pride for them as they are performing or being recognized in one way or another. It means so much to them, especially when we go out of our way and make a special effort to be present.

Sometimes, single parents (or both parents) who have more than one job say they *don't have time* to show up. But, as I said, kids understand legitimate reasons why a parent might not be able to make a game, a performance, etc. What they get sad about is when they know you are choosing not to be there. When you choose not to make time. It's not that we don't have time. Everybody has time. It's choosing to make time for our children that matters, and they know the difference when we choose not to, and when we choose to make time for them. What we choose to give our time to says a lot about our life priorities and the hero parent chooses to invest time in their children as a priority.

Integrity. We don't have to be perfect to be a hero; we just need to be honest. Integrity is key to winning the love and respect of our children.

I have had the blessing of having my children tell me or write about me as their hero. It is a very rewarding thing to hear and feel from your child. Yet, the thing is that I know the real me. My kids know the real me. And the real me is far from perfect. Nevertheless, they still consider me their hero. How can that be? It's simple really. What makes us heroes is not that we are perfect parents, but rather that we are honest parents. That we have integrity. That we own up to our mistakes and failures. We look our children in the eye when we have done the wrong thing, said the wrong thing, acted in a wrong way, and we sincerely apologize. That is how an imperfect parent can still be the hero of their children and win their loyalty.

Crisis. It may not seem like a crisis to us, but if it is important to them, in those hard times we are there for them. We may not have all the answers or know the right words to speak, but we can show up in the crisis of life and often that is all that is needed.

Throughout the lives of each of my children, I have watched them and experienced with them disappointment, failure, letdowns, heartbreak, and grief. It is one of the things about loving your children so much that is so painful because when they hurt . . . you hurt. Maybe even more at times because you never want to see your children sad, crying and broken-hearted for one reason or another. In that moment, you want to take their pain away. You want to take their place. You want to say and do the right thing to make it all better. But the reality is, you can't. But even if you can't take the pain away in the moment, you can be there; quietly, calmly, empathetically. They appreciate that. They always remember that, and it goes a long way in earning trust, respect, and loyalty.

In the case of my sons, it was usually after a disappointing loss in sports. For my daughters, it was usually a hard breakup, letdown, or betrayal of a boyfriend. In these sensitive and tough times, it's not our words so much as our presence that makes the difference.

Prevention from choosing a negative lifestyle is not a matter of keeping our children from ever being touched by any or every negative experience available in today's American culture. No, our challenge is not one of isolation, but one of infiltration. Infiltrating the hearts and homes of the hopeless with parent heroes!

CONCLUSION
The POM Stepparent Mindset

When I have watched presidential debates, one of the questions that often asked is: *What are you, as president, going to do about* . . . and then the debate moderators go on to name some pressing issue or problem in a city or a particular community: gun violence, rampant crime, gangs, public education, and the like. And the answer (or non-answer) is always the same: more laws, more police, more government, more regulations, etc. These questions and answers in my view continue to perpetuate these problems, not solve them.

First, the proposed solutions of more laws, more police, and more academic studies of social problems have proven to be ineffective for many years now. Secondly, politicians, i.e. the federal government, have never been the solution to solving community problems.

Thirdly, it is not the job of the president of the United States to provide solutions or be expected to fix the problems in local communities. That is not what we elect the president to do. Solving community problems is the job of state and local government in partnership with business, education, faith-based organizations, and parents of families. In other words, local problems need to be solved by the local community leaders, be they politicians, police, principals of schools, pastors, or volunteer parents.

The local citizens live there, work there, and care the most about what type of environment they and their families live in. They are in tune with and in touch with the heartbeat of the community. Given the opportunity and proper resources, local community leaders will resolve most community problems over time. To be sure, I'm not saying every single problem will always be completely solved. Solving community problems requires hard work, compassion, and leadership from dedicated individuals living in those neighborhoods.

I know of what I speak not only because I have done it myself, but also because after founding and being the executive director of a national nonprofit intermediary for twenty years, the Latino Coalition for Community Leadership, providing funding and capacity building to local faith and community-based nonprofits, I understand the nuances and difficulty of dealing with communities and healing individuals and families. Thus, I am not speaking from theory or suggesting a *pie in the sky* solution. But what I am saying is that it is a mistaken notion that the federal government and/or president of the United States should be expected to solve local community problems, and we must stop giving our citizens that expectation of the president.

All the above said, the most important element, force, and key to building healthy and safe communities are parents. And given the fact that single parents, stepparents and blended families have become the norm in our country, stepparents, in addition to biological parents, as well as foster parents and other child caregivers, have become the most important people to help both solve and prevent community problems. Why? Because our role and influence play a vital part for the future of the community. As I stated earlier, the neighbors in a neighborhood, the students in the schools, the entrepreneurs and employees of businesses, and citizens of the community come from the home. And therefore, who we send into the community every day is who we raise at home. The family, be it nuclear or otherwise, is our best and first line of defense against negative influences. The home is the best place for prevention and intervention governance of keeping communities healthy, happy, and safe.

I believe every era has those extraordinary men and woman who will rise to the challenges of their time. I wrote this book for you stepparents of blended families because it is my contention that you are the extraordinary men and woman of our time who must rise up to take on the complex challenges of this time, more than any other single entity, institution or community program. That's why I call you *Parents on a Mission!*

Notes

Introduction
1. John P. Hoffmann, "Family Structure, Unstructured Socializing, and Delinquent Behavior," *Journal of Criminal Justice* 87 (July 2023): 102086. https://doi.org/10.1016/j.jcrimjus.2023.102086.
2. Constance Ahrons, *The Good Divorce* (New York: HarperCollins e-Books), 2014.
3. Carolina Aragão, "The Modern American Family," Pew Research Center, September 14, 2023. https://www.pewresearch.org/social-trends/2023/09/14/the-modern-american-family/.
4. US Census Bureau, "America's Families and Living Arrangements: 2022," Census.gov, November 21, 2022. https://www.census.gov/data/tables/2022/demo/families/cps-2022.html.

Part One Before the Blend: Understanding the Emotional Realities of Stepparenting

Chapter 1. Unmatched and Unattached
1. Thomas E, . Gaddis and James O. Long, *PANZRAM, A Journal of Murder* (Los Angeles: (Amok)2002, 5, 6, 11, 12-15.
2. Katherine Siefert, *How Children Become Violent: Keeping Your Kids out of Gangs, Terrorist Organizations, and Cults* (Boston, Acanthus Publishing), 2007, 11-15.
3. Alice Miller, *The Drama of The Gifted Child: The Search for the True Self* (New York: Basic Books, 1997), 28-29.

4. *PANZRAM*, 14.
5. "Home - Child Trends." ChildTrends,. accessed February 18, 2025. https://mastresearchcenter.org/mast-center-research/defining-and-measuring-the-complexity-of-stepfamilies-in-the-united-states/.
6. Sophonisba Preston Breckinridge and Edith Abbot, *The Delinquent Child and the Home* (Hardpress Publishing, January 2013).

Chapter 2. No Voice—No Choice

1. "Becoming a stepparent has ruined my life," n.d. https://www.reddit.com/r/stepparents/comments/1cfm5ba/becoming_a_step_parent_has_ruined_my_life/.
2. "How to Help Your Child Accept a New Relationship," Very well mindset, October 5, 2024.
3. "When and How to Introduce Your Children to Your New Partner." Relationships Australia, NSW, October 29, 2023. 2. https://verywellmindset.com/how-to-help-your-child-accept-a-new-relationship/.
4. Avolyn Fisher, "I Grew up in a Broken Home but It Shaped Me and I'm Blessed for It," thoughtcatalog.com, 2014. https://thoughtcatalog.com/avolyn-fisher/2014/05/i-grew-up-in-a-broken-home-but-it-shaped-me-and-im-blessed-for-it/.

Chapter 3. Domestic Silence—Domestic Violence

1. Alice Miller. *Breaking Down the Walls of Silence: The Liberating Experience of Facing Painful Truth* (New York: Basic Books, 2009). 4.
2. Misic, Lidija. "Tackling the Issues of Violence against Children by Their Step-Parents." Humanium, May 2, 2023. https://www.humanium.org/en/tackling-the-issues-of-violence-against-children-by-their-step-parents/.
3. Richard R Ramos, *Parents on a Mission: How Parents Can Win the Competition for the Heart, Mind, and Loyalty of Their Children* (Parker: CO: Outskirts Press, 2023.)
4. Miller, *Breaking Down the Walls of Silence*, 57
5. Michael Kraut, "Domestic Violence in Nontraditional Families – Part 1," Los Angeles Criminal Defense Attorney Blog, June 24, 2021. https://www.losangelescriminaldefenseattorneyblog.com/domestic-violence-in-nontraditional-families-part-1/.

6. Agata Debowska, George Hales, and Daniel Boduszek, "Violence against Children by Stepparents," *The SAGE Handbook of Domestic Violence*, 2021, 553–69. https://doi.org/10.4135/9781529742343.n33.
7. Miller, *Breaking Down the Walls of Silence*, 33

Chapter 4. Mama Trauma
1. Peg Streep, "Chapter 1," in *Mean Mothers, Overcoming The Legacy of Hurt*, 1–16 (New York: HarperCollins), 2009.
2. "Your mental health and wellbeing | ready steady baby!" Accessed February 18, 2025. https://www.nhsinform.scot/ready-steady-baby/pregnancy/relationships-and-wellbeing-in-pregnancy/your-mental-health-and-wellbeing-in-pregnancy/.
3. Donna Ford and Linda Watson-Brown, *The Step Child: A True Story of a Broken Childhood*. (London: Vermilion, an imprint of Ebury), 2011.
4. Edwin H. Friedman, Margaret M. Treadwell, and Edward W. Beal. *A Failure of Nerve: Leadership in the Age of the Quick Fix* (New York: Church Publishing), 2017, 19.

Chapter 6. The Stepdad—Gap
1. Kyle V. Robinson, "What It's like to Be Abused by the Man Your Mom Wants You to Call 'Dad.'" The Mighty, June 17, 2024. https://themighty.com/topic/post-traumatic-stress-disorder-ptsd/stepfather-abuse/.

Chapter 7. The Blended Family Triangle
1. Friedman, 204.
2. Murray Bowen and Michael E. Kerr. *Family Evaluation*. (New York: W. W Norton and Company), 1988, p 134.

Part 2 POM Principles and The Stepparent's Role as a Transformational Leader

Chapter 9. Personal Growth for Stepparents – Managing Emotions and Expectations
1. Rose Fitzgerald Kennedy,. *Times to Remember* (New York: Doubleday), 1995.

2. Viktor E. Frankl, *Man's Search for Meaning: A Young Adult Edition* (Boston: Beacon Press Books), 2017.

Chapter 10. Earning Respect as a Stepparent – Balancing Authority and Influence

1. Lindsay C. Gibson, *Adult Children of Emotionally Immature Parents: How to Heal from Distant, Rejecting, or Self-involved Parents*. (New Harbinger Publishers, 2015)
2. Gordon Neufeld and Gabor Maté, *Hold on to Your Kids: Why Parents Need to Matter More than Peers* (New York: Ballantine Books), 2024, x.
3. D. Baumrind, "Parenting styles and adolescent development," in J. Brooks-Gunn, R. M. Lerner, and A. C. Petersen (Eds.), *The Encyclopedia on Adolescence* (New York: Garland Publishing, 1991), 746-758.

Chapter 11. The Home Field Advantage – Building Strong Attachment That Counter External Influences

1. Miller, *The drama of The gifted child*, 28-29.
2. https://www.first5california.com/en-us/

Chapter 12. Discipline with Love and Fairness – Avoiding the Authoritarian Style of Parenting

3. James Dobson, *Dare to Discipline* (Carol Stream: IL: Tyndale House), 1970.

Chapter 14. Reconciliation in Blended Families – The Power of Forgiveness and Unconditional Love

1. The King James Bible. *The Gospel of Luke*. Chapter 15.

Chapter 15. How Stepparents Win Loyalty – Leading Your Blended Family to Success

1. Jillian Peterson and James A. Densley, *The Violence Project: How to Stop a Mass Shooting Epidemic* (New York: Abrams Press, 2022). 115.

Acknowledgments

Writing this book has been a deeply personal journey, one made possible by the support and encouragement of many. I am especially grateful to Steven Harrison and his Get Published Now Team: my writing coach, Sarah Brown, whose guidance, wisdom, and belief in my vision helped bring this book to life, Cristina Smith, Valerie and Scott Costa, Christy Day, and Shannon Hazel. To my wife and children, for their patience and understanding as we have navigated the challenges of stepparenting our blended family, and to the stepparents and families I've had the pleasure of serving over the years, whose stories and experiences helped shape this work. Finally, to all those who believe in the power of love, growth, forgiveness, and reconciliation, this book is for you. Thank you for being part of this journey.

About the Author

Richard is an author, speaker, and parent coach with over thirty years of experience in leadership development, family dynamics, and community building. He has made a significant national and international impact through his work with high-risk youth, parents, and families, creating safe, supportive environments for personal growth and community transformation. Richard has trained over 2,000 parent mentors through his innovative leadership curriculum and has authored several books, including *Parents on a Mission* and *From the Margins to the Mainstream—Preparing Latino Youth for Leadership in the Twenty-First Century*.

As a recognized expert in preventing community violence and fostering positive family environments, Richard brings a unique blend of personal experience and professional insight to his work. His passion for helping families navigate the challenges of stepparenting and build meaningful connections within their homes has reached communities across the globe. Through his coaching, training, and writing, Richard empowers individuals to lead with confidence and create lasting change in both their families and communities. His mission is clear: to help families not just survive but thrive in a world that demands resilience and connection.

For more information, resources, and a free video series about Parents on a Mission visit: www.richardrramos.com.

www.ingramcontent.com/pod-product-compliance
Lightning Source LLC
Chambersburg PA
CBHW051942290426
44110CB00015B/2076